Plaid Cats:
The Best of Their Breeds

By
David J. Sheskin

Published in the United States and the United Kingdom
by WingSpan Press, Livermore, CA

The WingSpan name, logo and colophon are the trademarks of WingSpan Publishing.

ISBN 978-1-59594-577-8

First edition 2016

Printed in the United States of America

www.wingspanpress.com

Library of Congress Control Number: 2016935988

1 2 3 4 5 6 7 8 9 10

Table of Contents

The Fifty Plaid Cats Breeds and the Winning Cat

The Fifty Plaid Cats Breeds and the Winning Cat

Breed 26: Perfume (Marmalade)
Breed 27: Velvet (Decadence)
Breed 28: Warrior (Cha-Cha)
Breed 29: Sphinx (Caesar)
Breed 30: Casanova (Lord Byron)
Breed 31: Magnolia (Gladys)
Breed 32: Whirligig (Topspin)
Breed 33: Neon (Halo)
Breed 34: Lupine (Foxy)
Breed 35: Leprechaun (Shamrock)
Breed 36: Cyclone (Jellyroll)
Breed 37: Pearl of Kashmir (Tutti-Fruitti)
Breed 38: Sugarcane (Candy)
Breed 39: Mediterranean (Domino)
Breed 40: Peekaboo (Confucius)
Breed 41: Firecracker (Sparkles)
Breed 42: African Rainbow (Lollipop)
Breed 43: Belle (Scarlet)
Breed 44: Wanderer (Hobo)
Breed 45: Rio (Tarzan)
Breed 46: Iceberg (Snowflake)
Breed 47: Behemoth (Samson)
Breed 48: Neptune (Shark)
Breed 49: Cricket (Belly Button)
Breed 50: Dappled Blue (Rascal)

Introduction

Explore the fascinating and colorful world of plaid cats. Numbered among the most magnificent creatures in all of nature, these exotic felines were developed by visionary ailurophiles in order to gratify the aesthetic sensibilities of those who are fascinated by both cats and color. The cats in this book are the most recent winners of the "**best of their breeds**" competition — an annual affair attended by a select few who have become privy to the world of plaid cats. But now **you** can experience the beauty and whimsy of plaid cats! So, dear cat lover, begin the visual feast!

Plaid

Any of a large number of patterns employed for textiles in which there are stripes of assorted colors and widths crossed at right angles that are set upon a solid background.

Cats

Any of several carnivores of the family *Felidae*, such as the domestic cat, lion, tiger, leopard, jaguar, cougar, wildcat, lynx and cheetah.

BREED 1: OUTBACK

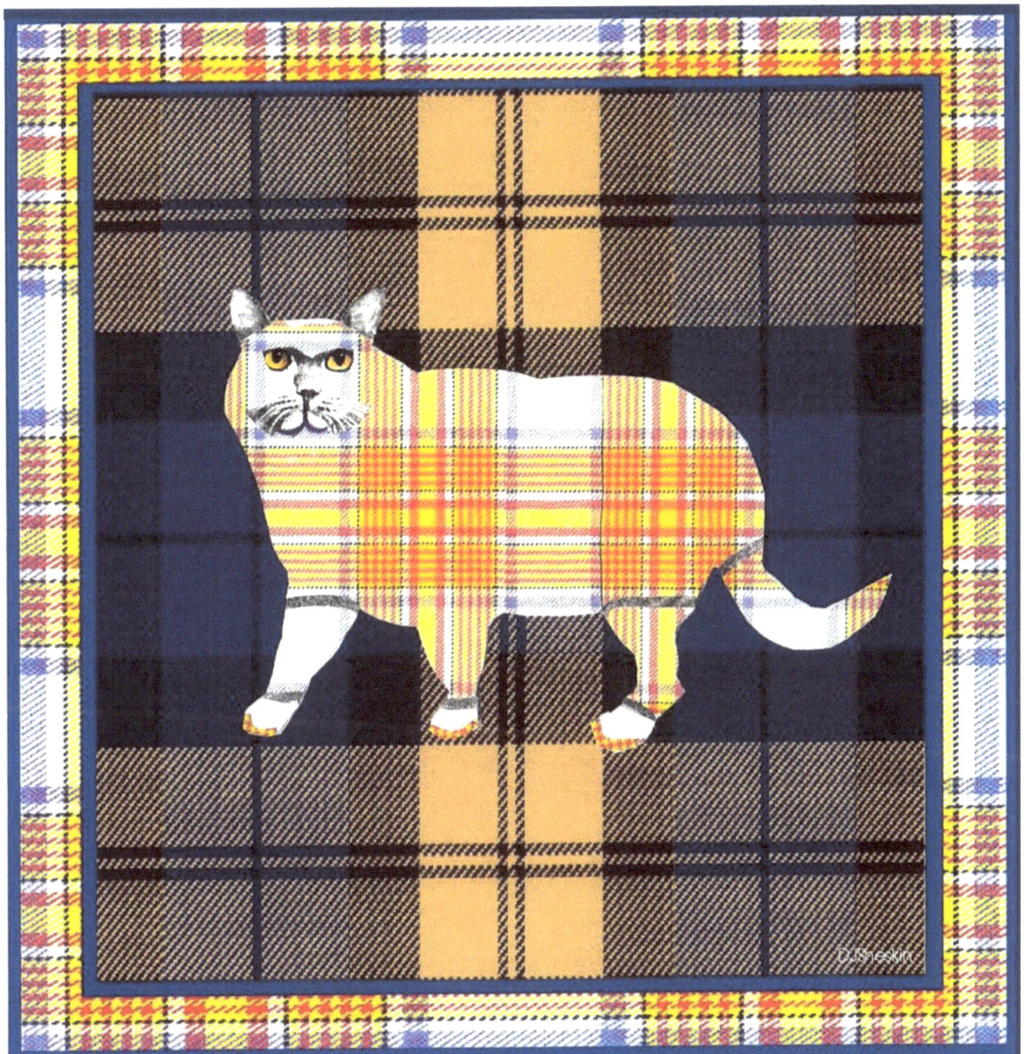

Breed 1: **Outback**
Best of Breed: *Butterscotch*

The *Outback* is a working cat from the mountainous regions of Western Australia. Its body is massive and powerful. Males may weigh as much as 30 pounds with wide shoulders and a stocky neck. The fur of the *Outback*, although thick and dense, is surprisingly silky. These cats thrive living outdoors and enjoy the companionship of other animals. An exceptional mouser, the *Outback* is an adept hunter who subsists on a diet of birds, snakes, mice and other small mammals.

BREED 2: PETIT-PLAID

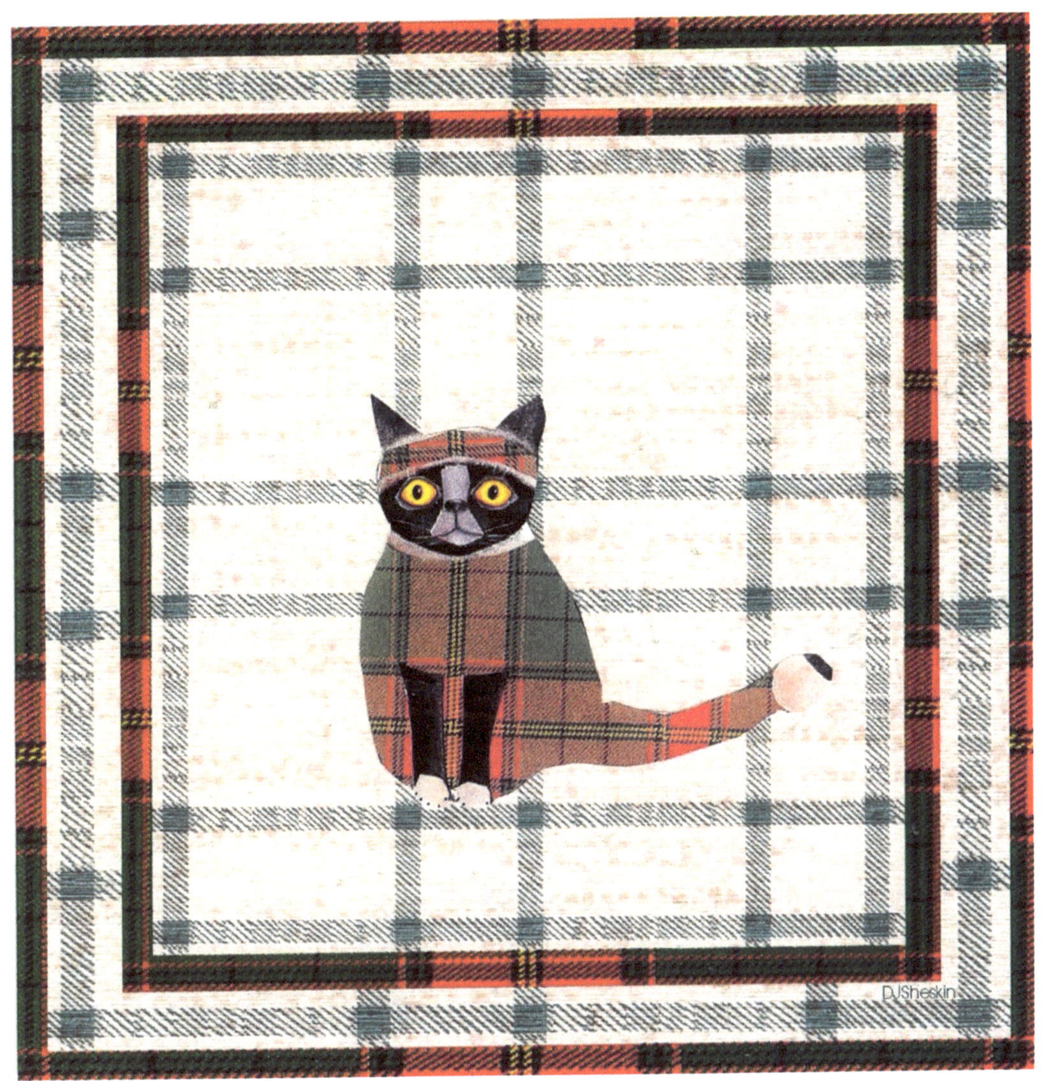

Breed 2: **Petit Plaid**
Best of Breed: *Bon-Bon*

The *Petit Plaid* breed is manmade, having resulted from cross breeding a number of now extinct miniature plaid breeds. Rarely exceeding six inches in length, the *Petit Plaid* is among the most affectionate of feline species. Bred to live indoors and inclined to sleep excessively, this cat has a very small appetite, probably because its sedentary lifestyle requires minimal caloric intake. When it does eat, it favors herbs such as licorice and nutmeg, as well as pungent cheeses such as cheddar and Limburger. It seems to enjoy life most with a single person who shares its respect for peace and quiet.

BREED 3: ROMAN

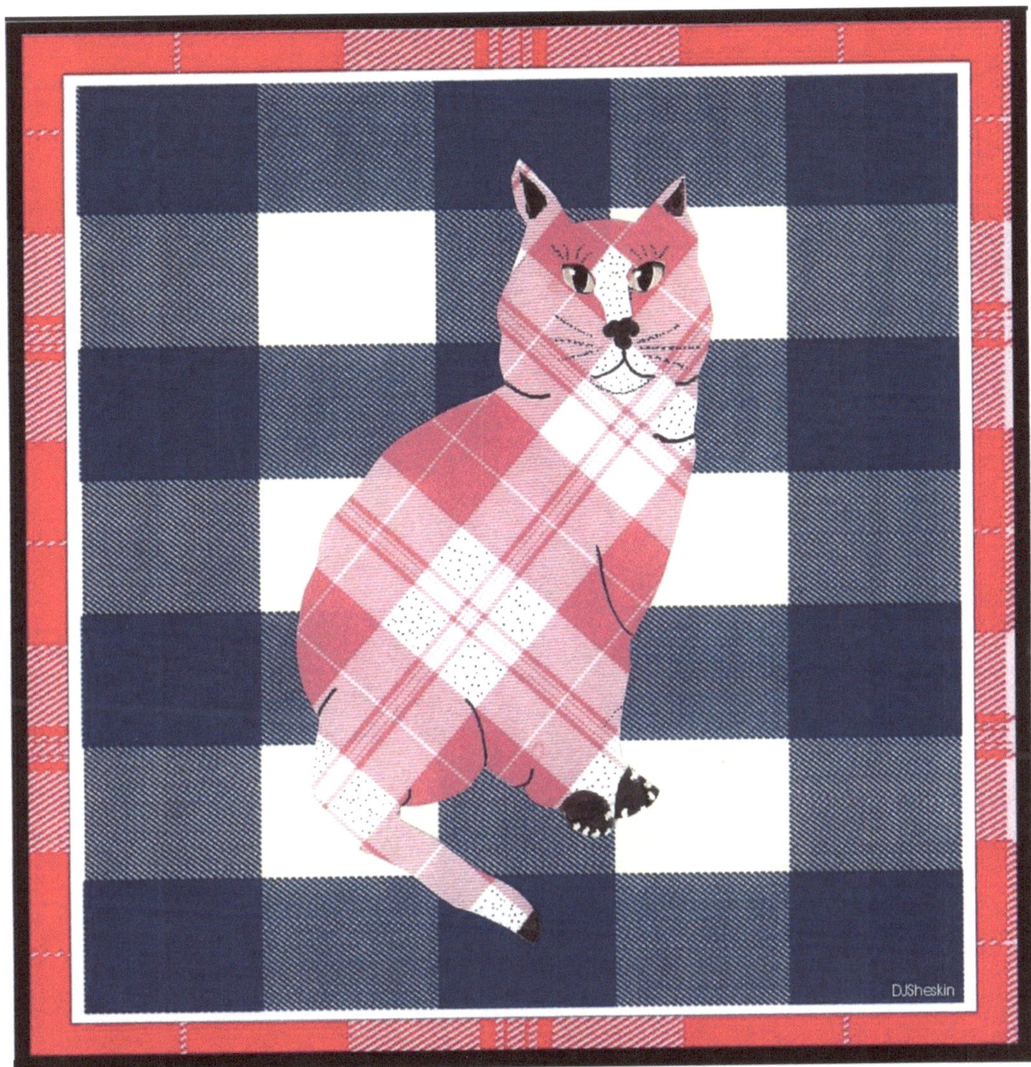

Breed 3: **Roman (Queen)**
Best of Breed: *Cleopatra*

The name *Roman Queen* is generally only employed for the female of this breed who is both a stunning and emotional creature. Three-quarters or more of the offspring in a typical litter (which generally consists of 6 to 8 kittens) are females. Males of the breed (who are usually referred to as *Roman Kings*) have blue markings of varying intensities replacing the red tones found on the female. To minimize the emotional reactivity of the *Roman Queen*, it is recommended that this cat be handled gently but regularly from infancy. Under no circumstances should catnip or other preparations which have an excitatory effect on the nervous system be given to these highly emotional animals, since they can provoke fatal cardiac arrhythmias. Although *Roman Queens* do best on a bland diet that consists of rice, mashed potato, and assorted grains, they enjoy occasional treats consisting of marmalade, jello, and shredded coconut.

BREED 4: MAJESTIC

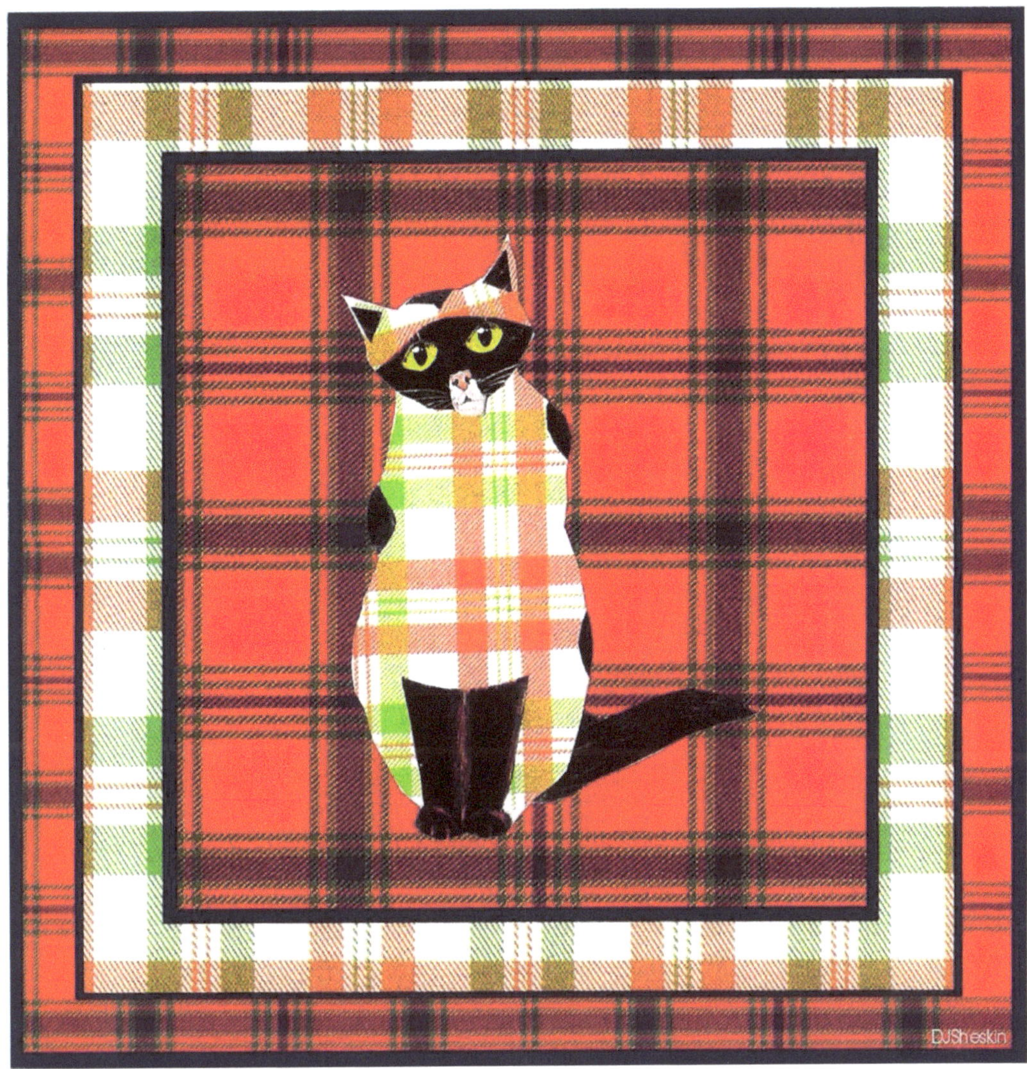

Breed 4: **Majestic**
Best of Breed: *Princess*

The *Majestic* is long and svelte with short, fine textured fur. These cats crave human attention and are quite assertive at getting it. The nomadic tribes of Mongolia have long regarded the *Majestic* as a good luck cat. Periodic rubbing with a gloved hand is recommended to maintain the vibrancy of the breed's chartreuse and red coat. The vocalizations of the *Majestic* are unique in that they are unusually melodious, often being compared with the tonality of a flute. This cat is a finicky eater that is partial to herbs such as basil, clove, burdock, ginger and fennel. It is, however, highly allergic to chocolate and other sweets. The *Majestic* is numbered among those breeds who have won the most ribbons at cat shows.

BREED 5: COSSACK

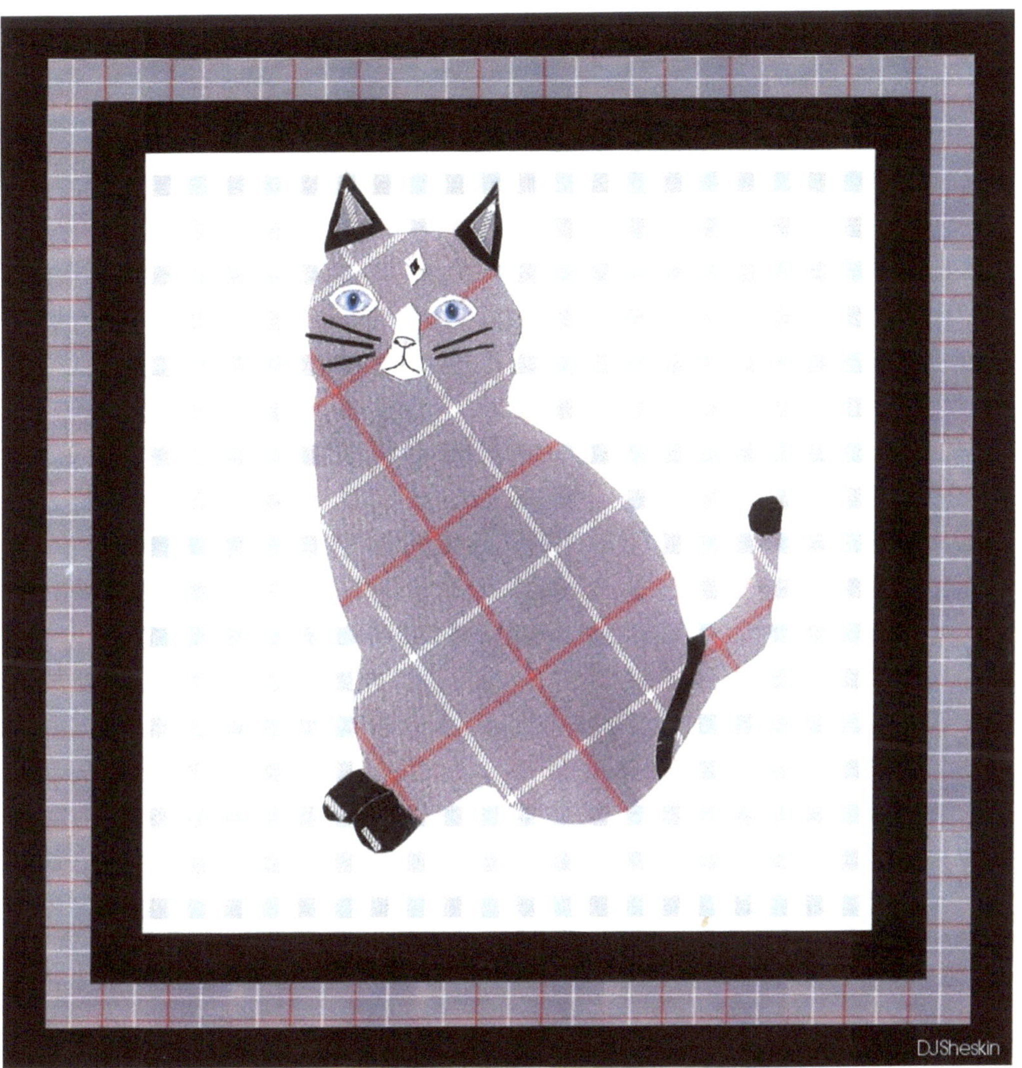

Breed 5: **Cossack**
Best of Breed: *Solitaire*

A distant relative of the *Russian blue*, the *Cossack* is a shy and quiet creature that prefers to spend most of its time alone. Increasingly popular as a show cat, the fur of this breed is like that of a plush-covered toy. A pregnant queen will generally have litters of eight to ten kittens, with three-quarters of them being males. Aside from primary sexual characteristics, the distinguishing feature between sexes is that males have pink eyes while females have blue eyes. Since the *Cossack* is unusually susceptible to respiratory problems, it should be maintained in a pollution free environment. The preferred diet of the *Cossack* are mild cheeses such as Gouda, Edam, and Ricotta. These cats also enjoy quenching their thirst with melted sherbet and assorted fruity wines, especially apricot and gooseberry.

BREED 6: NUTTY MIX

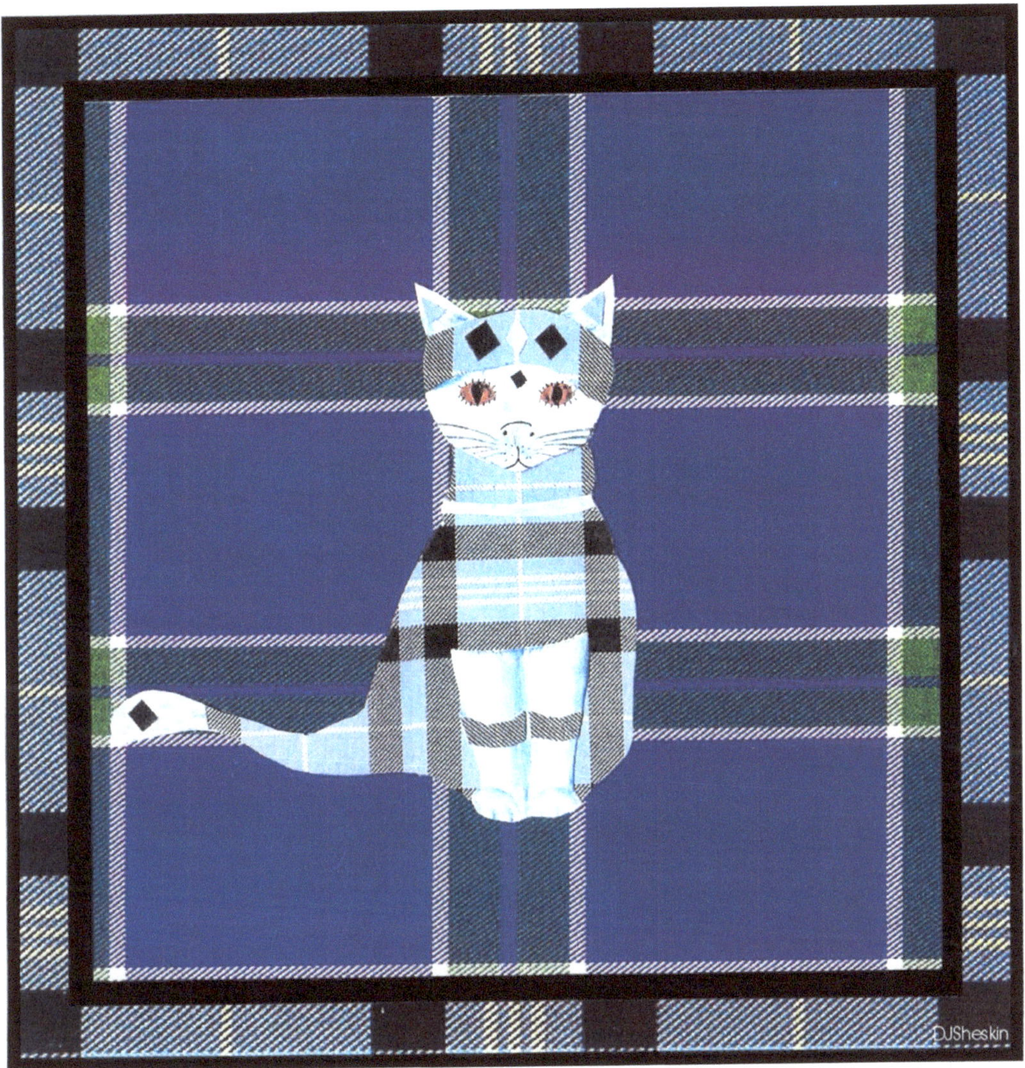

Breed 6: **Nutty Mix**
Best of Breed: *Peanut*

The *Nutty Mix* is a hybrid, the result of crossing the now all but extinct *Walnut* with the *Chestnut*. Retaining the best characteristics of the latter breeds, the typical *Nutty Mix* is precocious and extremely intelligent. Extremely small in stature (rarely exceeding a length of 8 inches), individuals of this breed are very talkative and tend to follow their owner almost like a dog, all the while vocalizing their desires as well as expressing their frustrations. A meticulous groomer, the *Nutty Mix* has a calm disposition, and is quite amenable to living with other cats. Not finicky eaters, the *Nutty Mix* will eat virtually any meat, fish, fowl, assorted fruits and vegetables, and, of course, chestnuts

BREED 7: PATRIOT

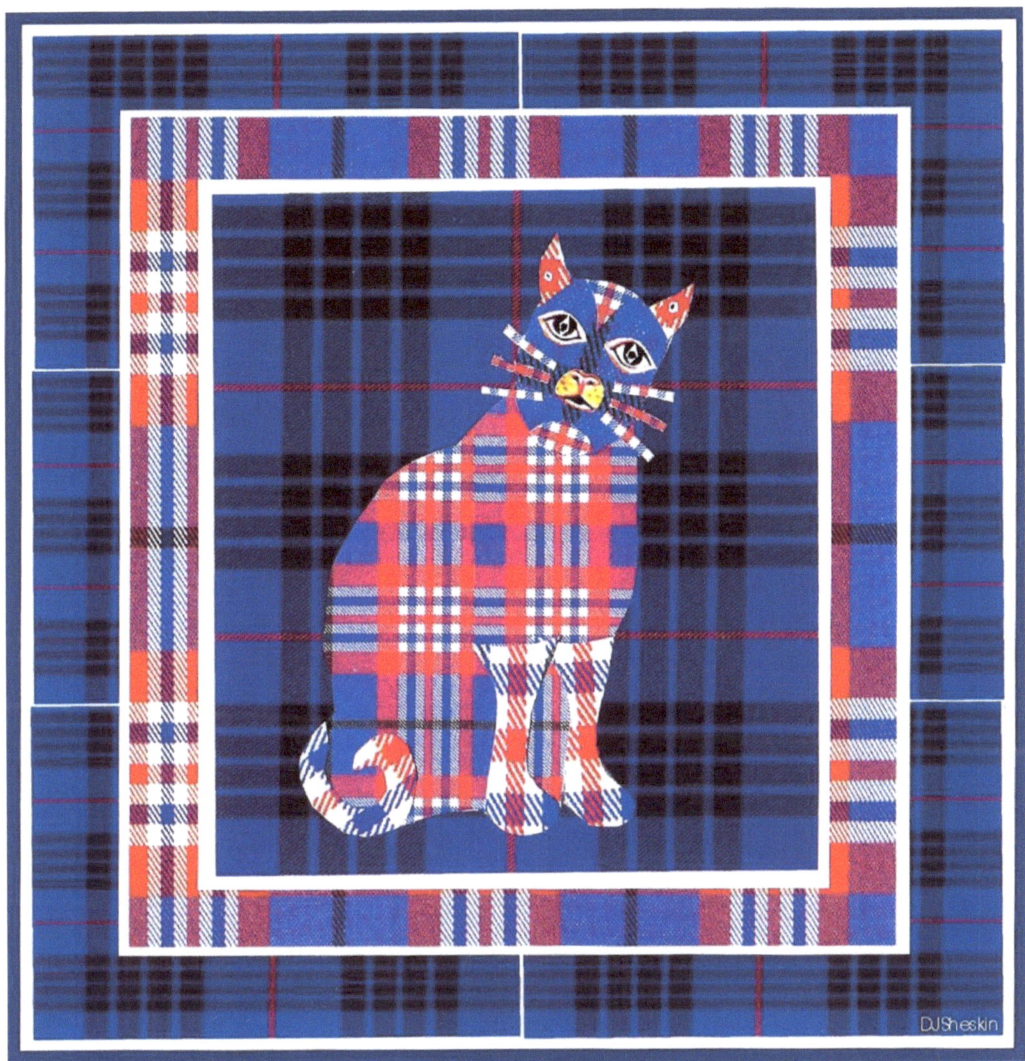

Breed 7: **Patriot**
Best of Breed: *Liberty*

Except for its brownish-yellow muzzle, this stunning cat is decorated in a magnificent coat of red, white and blue. The fur of the *Patriot* is thick and plush and the body is firm and well muscled. Typical of this breed are its boundless energy, intelligence, and independence. Although able to achieve a reasonable level of comfort living indoors, these cats are happiest when they have access to the outdoors. In the United States the *Patriot* is among the most popular of the plaid cats, and over the years has won many prizes at the most prestigious cat shows. Although the *Patriot* is not a finicky eater, its ideal daily menu would consist of a hamburger, a hot dog, corn and the cob, and slice of apple pie, all washed down with a warm glass of milk.

BREED 8: PLAIDICO

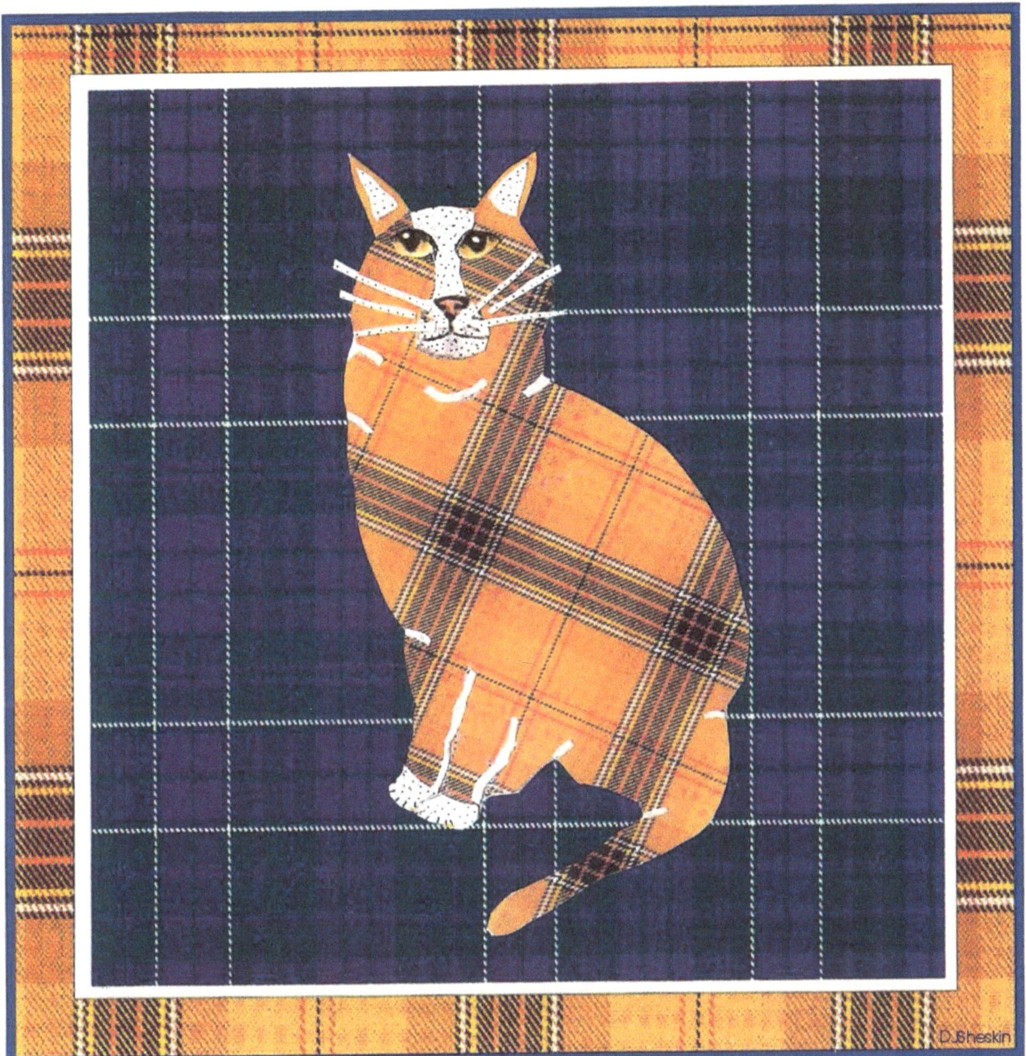

Breed 8: **Plaidico**
Best of Breed: *Buffy*

This hardy breed thrives in both an indoor and outdoor environment. Exhibiting a high tolerance for small children and other animals, the *Plaidico* is an ideal pet for the large family. Because of its firm, muscular body and lustrous coat, as well as the fact that it is both cooperative and responsive when handled by humans, the *Plaidico* is among the most popular of the plaid breeds displayed at shows. Its preferred diet consists of seafood such as mackerel, tuna, shrimp, sardines, and crab. A typical litter yields four to six kittens, with both the male and female being attentive parent.

BREED 9: HARLEQUIN

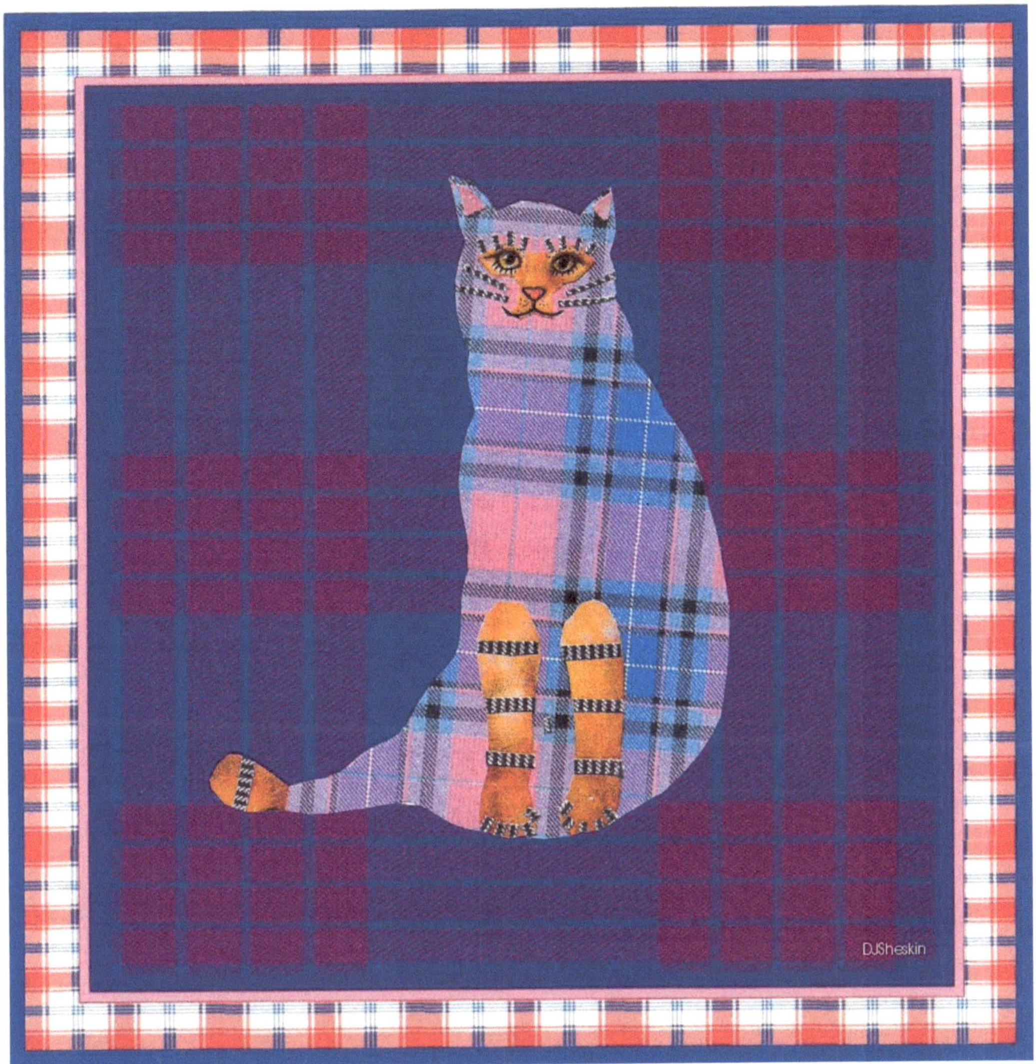

Breed 9: **Harlequin**
Best of Breed: *Juliet*

Although perfectly suited for an outdoor existence, this beautiful breed easily adjusts to the comforts of indoor living. Coveted by collectors because of its mellow disposition and exceptional coloration, the *Harlequin* is one of the most popular breeds among plaid cat owners. *Harlequins* have a preference for sharing a household with one or more cats or small dogs. A prolific breeder, females can produce a litter of ten of more kittens. Since females are open to mating with great frequency, they must be monitored very closely. Although not particularly finicky eaters, *Harlequins* are especially fond of French toast, cheese soufflé, and fruit cocktail.

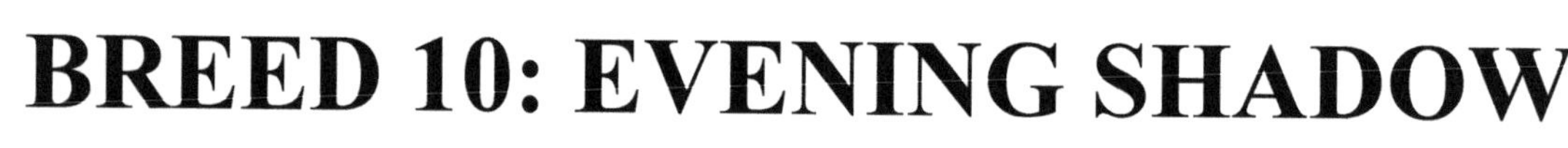

BREED 10: EVENING SHADOW

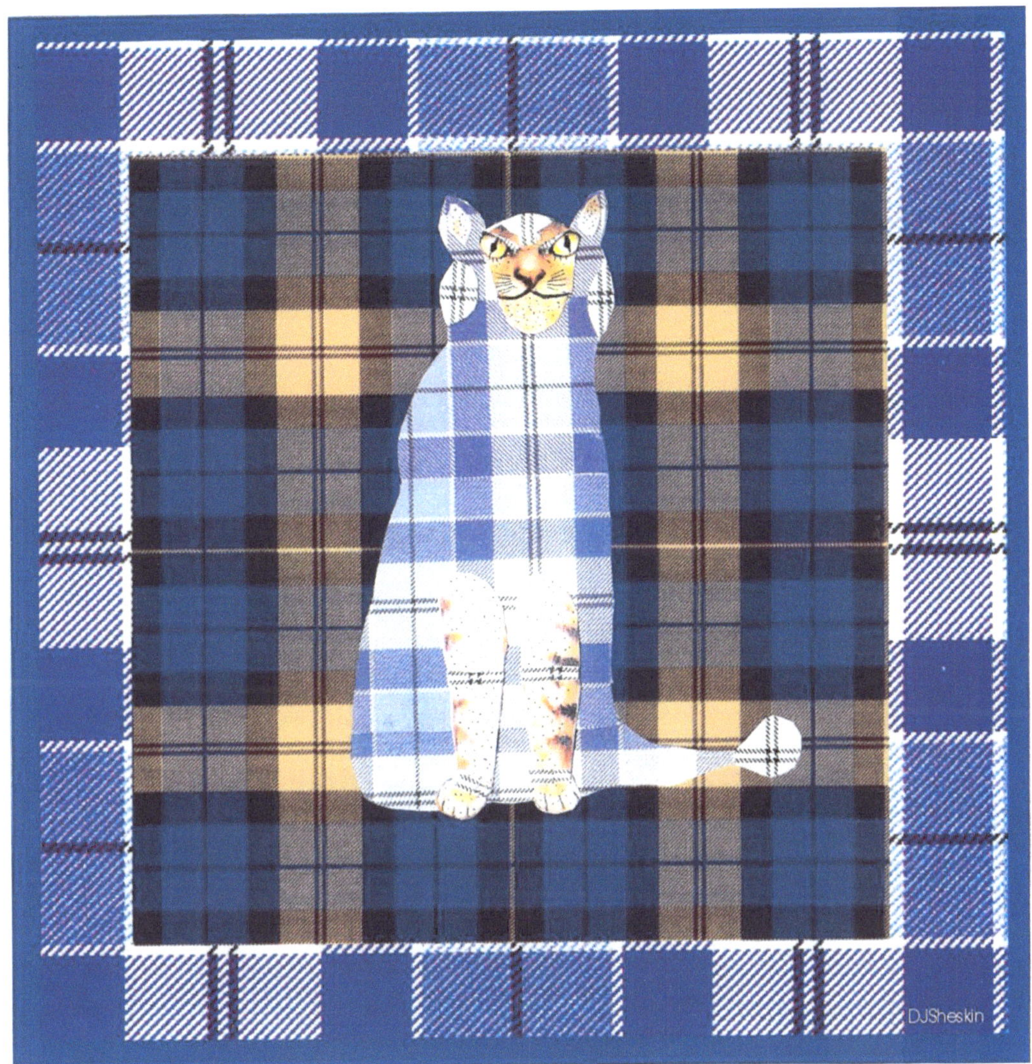

Breed 10: **Evening Shadow**
Best of Breed: *Moonbeam*

The *Evening Shadow* is the ideal companion for the older person. Sedentary and requiring minimal attention, this cat enjoys spending most of its time lounging at the feet of a human companion. Both the vocalizations and purr of this breed are unique — the vocalizations are a deep bass and the purr highly pitched. An idiosyncrasy of the *Evening Shadow* is that its firmly muscled body goes limp when it is picked up. *Evening Shadows* prefer not having to share a household with other animals. The preferred diet of this breed consists of delicatessen meats — most notably, pastrami, corned beef, tongue, and smoked turkey.

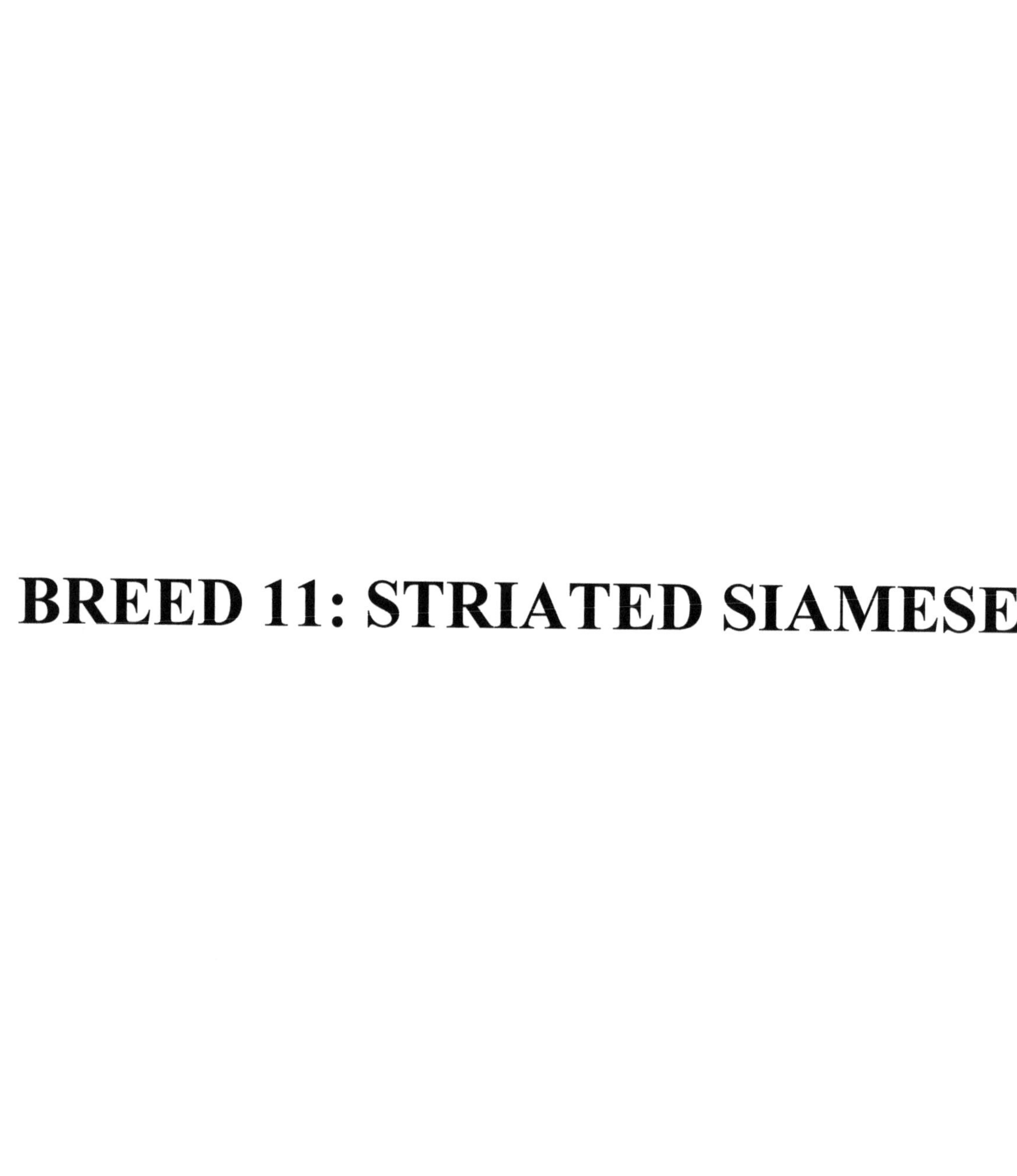

BREED 11: STRIATED SIAMESE

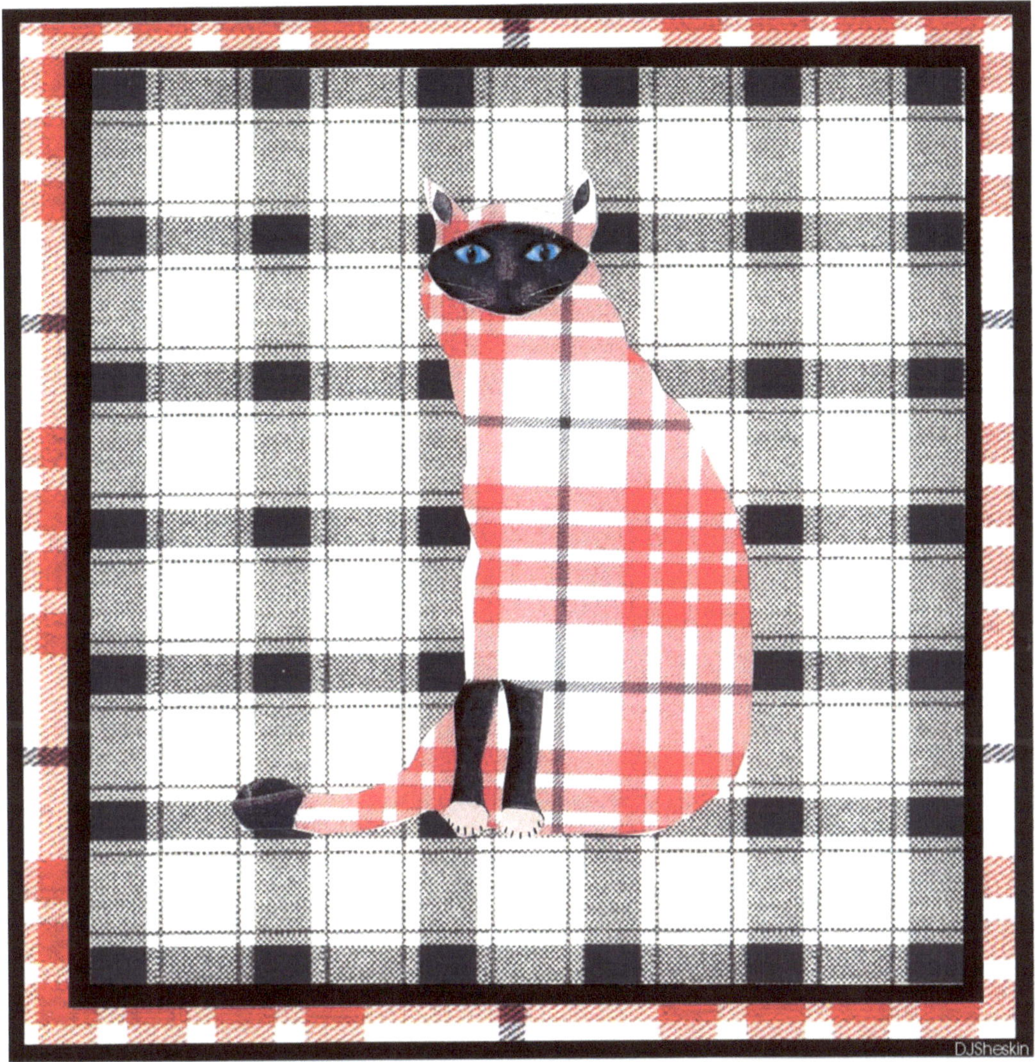

Breed 11: **Striated Siamese**
Best of Breed: *Delilah*

The *Striated Siamese* is the result of selective inbreeding of red and white feral plaid felines indigenous to the jungles of New Guinea with purebred *Siamese* cats. Among the most intelligent of the felines, the *Striated Siamese* is extremely talkative, inquisitive, and enterprising. Individuals of this breed exhibit exceptional devotion to their owners, as well as other people with whom they develop familiarity. Litters of three or four kittens are born to attentive parents who spend a considerable amount of time playing with their offspring. Finicky eaters, the *Striated Siamese* prefers gourmet meats topped with jams and nuts.

BREED 12: MAGISTRATE

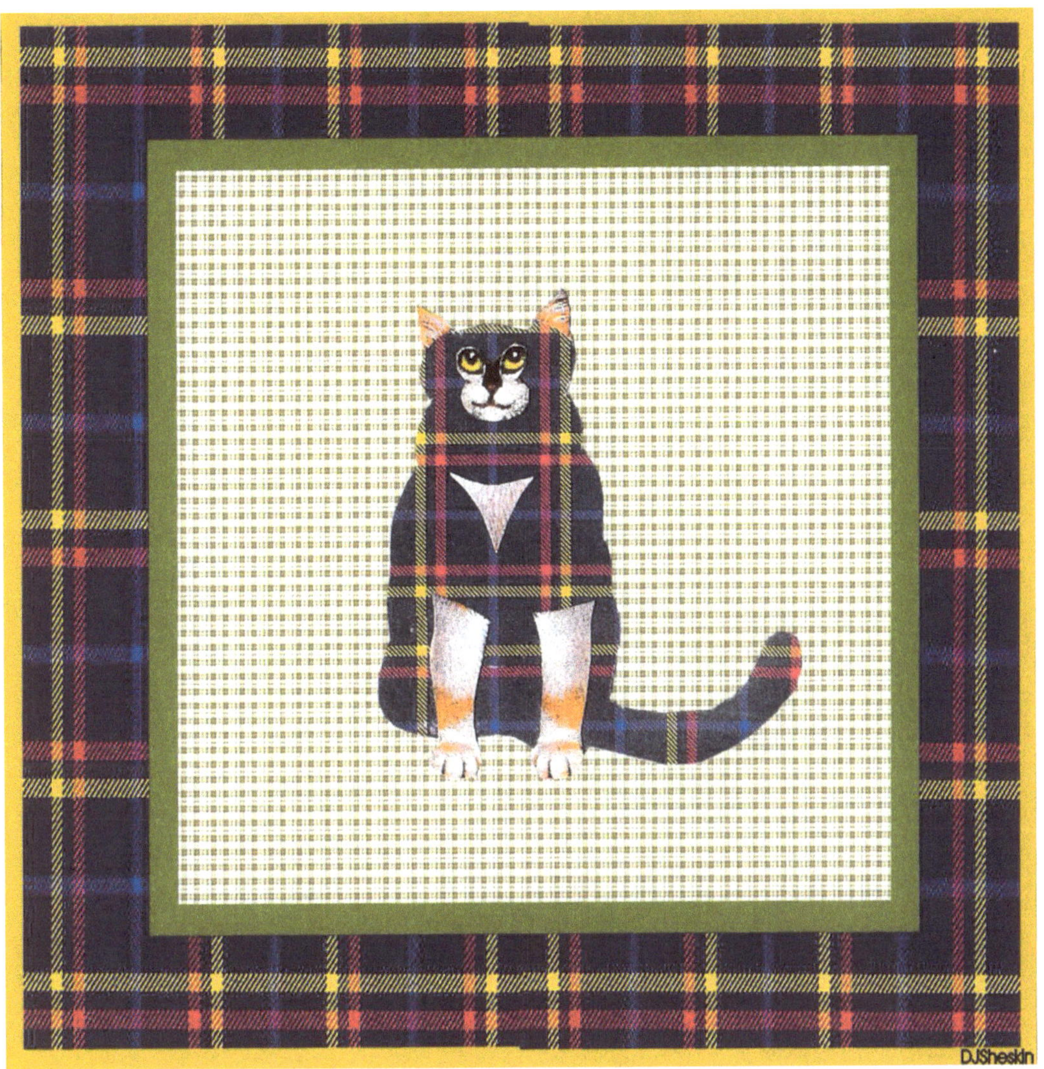

Breed 12: **Magistrate**
Best of Breed: *Emperor*

A dominant and assertive breed, a *Magistrate* will inevitably rule a household that is comprised of two or more cats representing different breeds. Regal in appearance, as well as in the way it carries itself, the *Magistrate* is affectionate with its human owners so long as it is accorded preferential treatment. Among the most intelligent of cats, the *Magistrate* can be taught to perform certain tricks, and because of this it is known as one of the most entertaining breeds. A finicky eater, the *Magistrate* is happiest with a diet that consists of caviar, smoked salmon, poached lobster, and fruit tarts.

BREED 13: PACIFIST

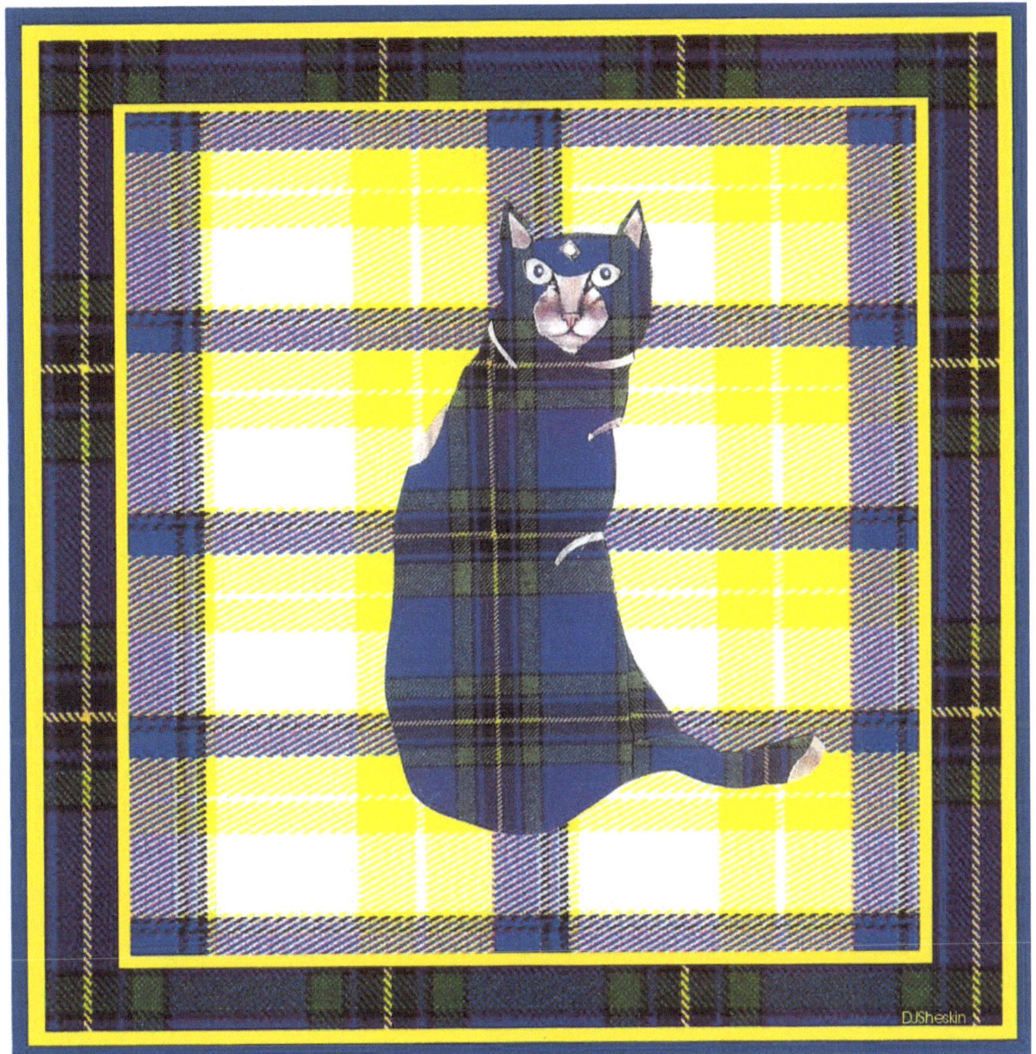

Breed 13: **Pacifist**
Best of Breed: *Gandhi*

Among the most coveted of the plaid cats, the *Pacifist* is renowned for its sweet disposition and tolerance for all living creatures. This breed spends most of its time curled up in a favorite spot (usually its owner's lap or favorite chair) either sleeping or contemplating its environment. Unlike other felines, it does not get excited by the presence of other creatures, large or small. Indeed, the *Pacifist* is even immune to effects of catnip. Among the most intelligent of the felines, this magnificent cat subsists on a diet of vegetables and nuts, and rejects all forms of meat, fish, and fowl.

BREED 14: MONOCHROME

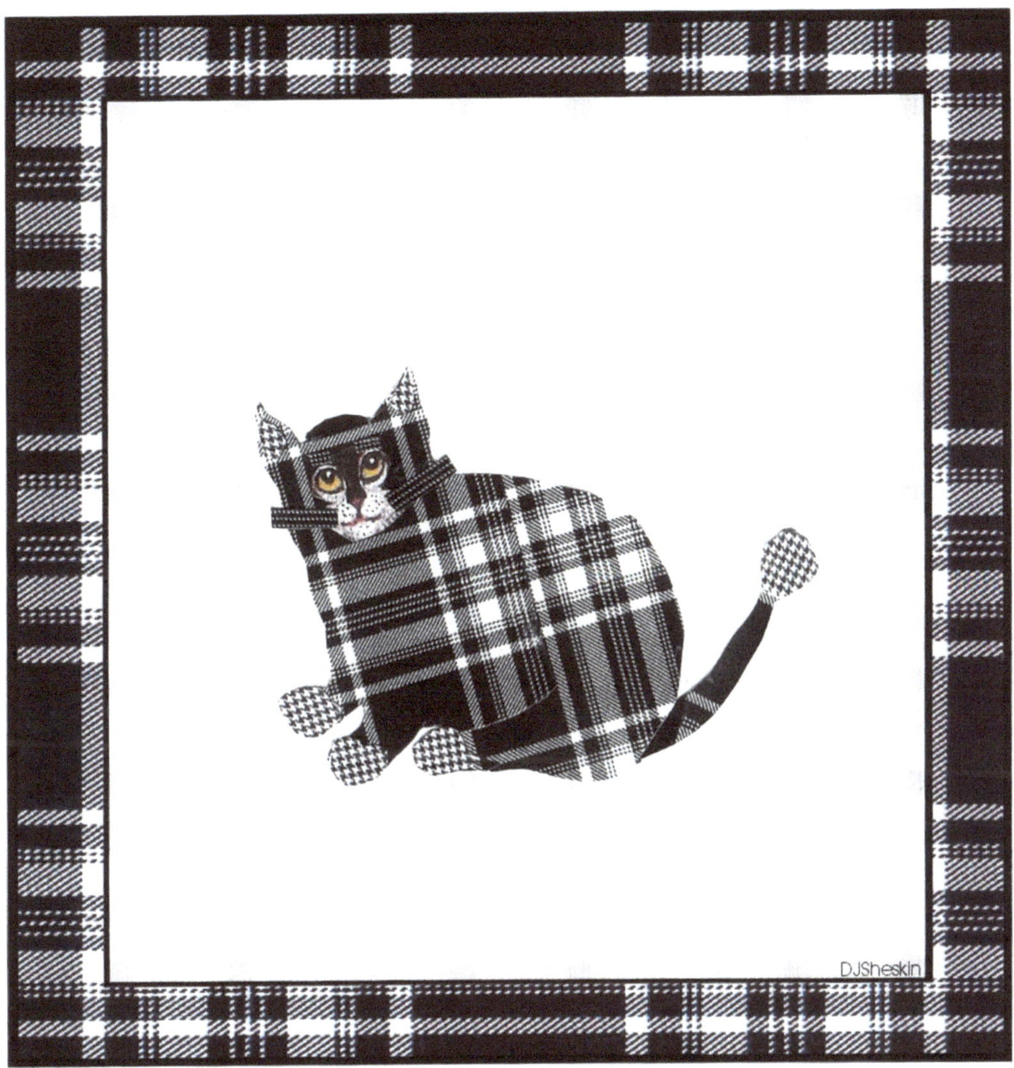

Breed 14: **Monochrome**
Best of Breed: *Licorice*

Unlike any of the other black and white breeds, the *Monochrome* is remarkable for its unique plaid coat. There appears to be a genetic link between eye color and deafness in these animals. Cats with golden eyes have normal hearing, while those born with green eyes (more commonly males) are completely deaf. The unusual tile effect that characterizes the paws, tail tip, and ears of the *Monochrome* is unique among the plaid breeds. The body of these extremely attractive animals, although compact, is not particularly well muscled. Because of the latter, *Monochrome* are prone to sustaining impact injuries to their limbs as a result of jumping. These cats are excellent house pets and enjoy human companionship. Attentive parents, both the male and female are conscientious in ministering to their kittens. The *Monochrome* is partial to seafood such as sardines, shrimp, and crab. It should be noted that these cats are extremely allergic to certain herbs, most notably marjoram, larkspur, and juniper.

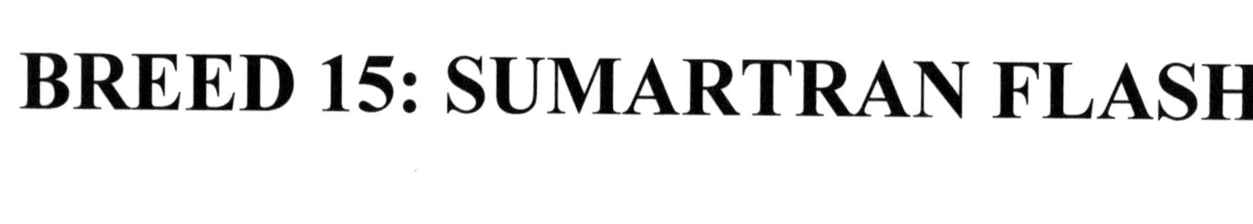

BREED 15: SUMARTRAN FLASH

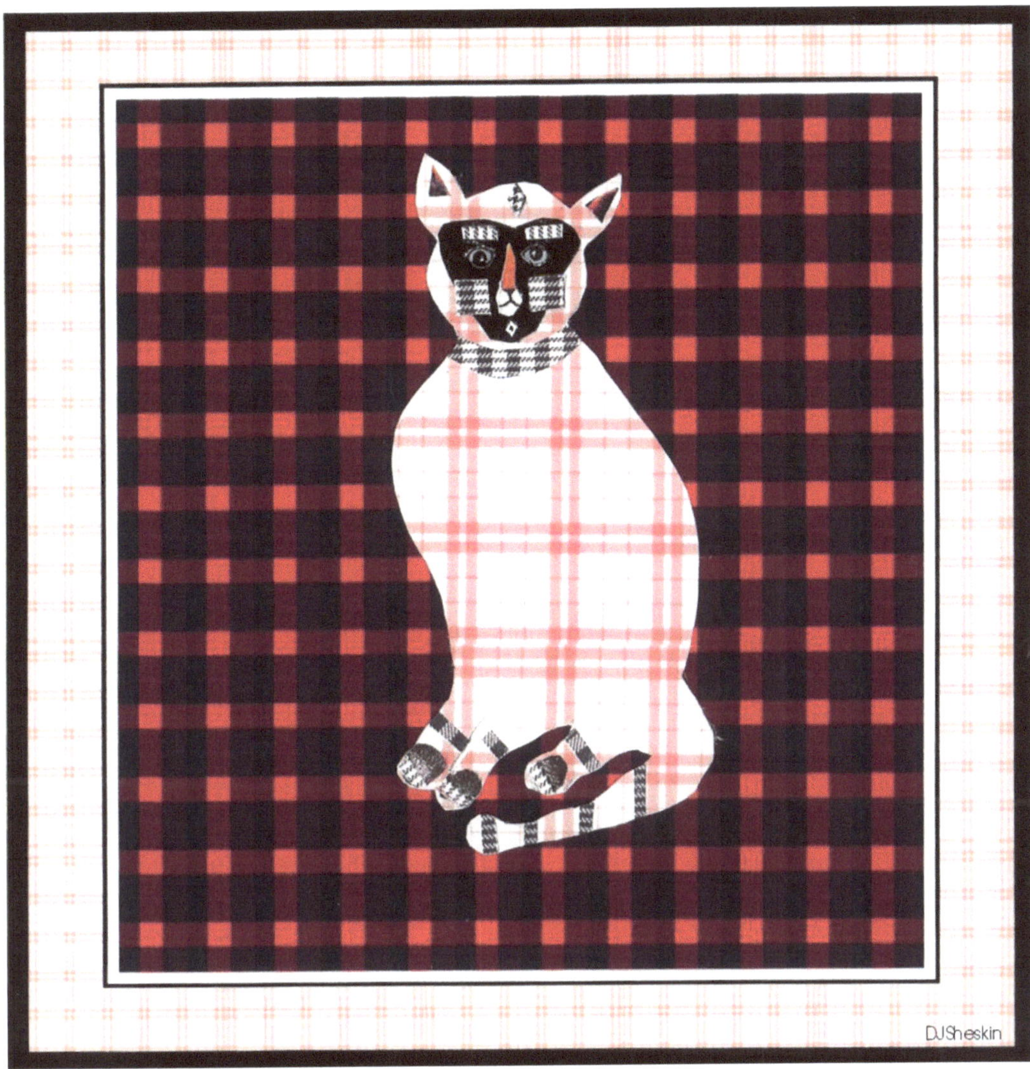

Breed 15: **Sumatran Flash**
Best of Breed: *Jellybean*

So named because of its insatiable appetite for jellybeans, this unusual breed with a heart-shaped head, is prized among collectors. Clocked at speeds of over 80 mph, the *Sumatran Flash* can outrun any known species. Because of its hyperactive nature, the *Sumatran Flash* is happiest living in an open outdoor environment where it is free to burn off the tremendous amount of energy that is packed into its small body. Because of its disinclination to confinement, most members of the breed live in the wild, and the few that have been domesticated are found on large rubber plantations owned by wealthy landowners in Sumatra and New Guinea. Aside from jellybeans, this breed subsists on a diet of hemp, vanilla beans, sweet potatoes, and okra.

BREED 16: TRICKSTER

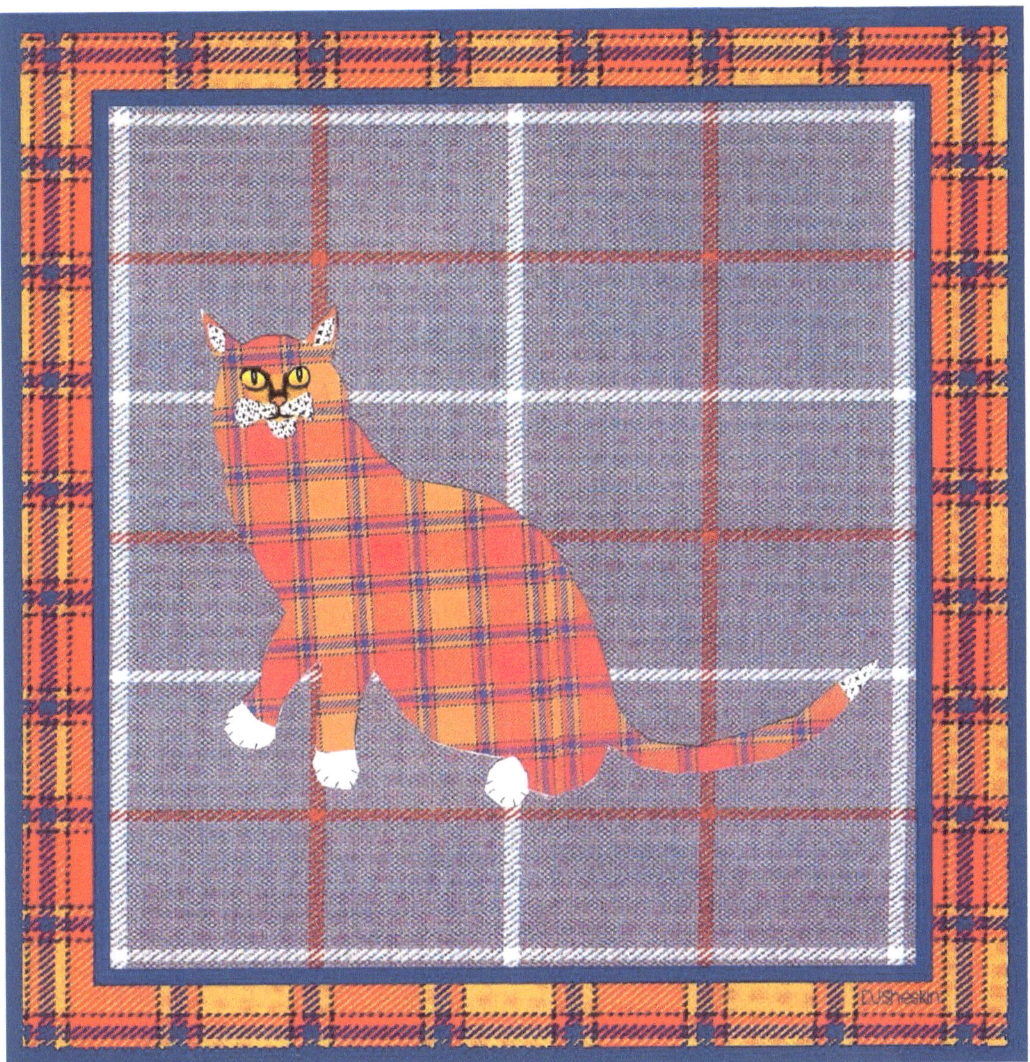

Breed 16: **Trickster**
Best of Breed: *Sneakers*

Aside from its beautiful plaid coat, the most striking aspect of this unusual breed is its solid white paws. Because of their blunt edged teeth and uncanny hunting ability, the *Trickster* is able to snare butterflies and moths without damaging the delicate body and wings of its prey. As a result of the latter, these cats are prized by lepidopterists, as well as collectors of other types of insects. Because of their peculiar dentition, the *Trickster* is partial to soft foods such as puddings and sherbets, as well as concentrated beverages that are high in protein. Although happiest when it has access to the outdoors, the *Trickster* is most content to spend its quiet time in an indoor environment where it is pampered and smothered with affection by one or more human companions.

BREED 17: SWEET-TOOTH

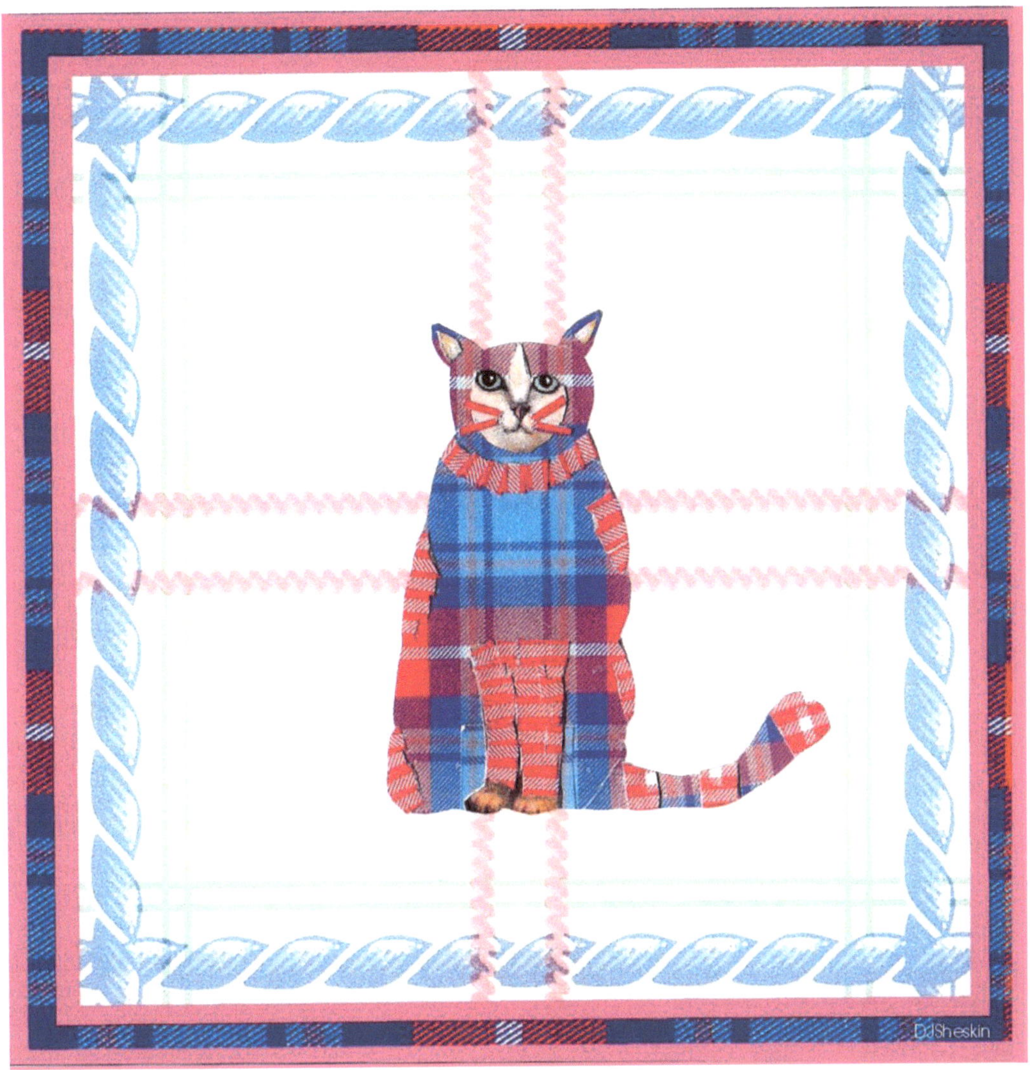

Breed 17: **Sweet-Tooth**
Best of Breed: *Peppermint*

Noted for its distinctive oval shaped head and the prominent crimson and blue markings that decorate its muscular body, the *Sweet-Tooth* is so named because of the sweet pungent odor that emanates from its sweat glands. Legend has it that the breed was developed in the early 1800s in catteries owned by the Sultan of Brunei to serve as companions to the members of his harem. Unusually friendly and assertive, a *Sweet-Tooth* will think nothing of jumping into your lap or onto your shoulder if it craves attention. When hungry, it often vigorously rubs its paw along its owner's leg. The preferred diet of the *Sweet-Tooth* consists of chocolate covered almonds, eggnog, and cinnamon coated raisins.

BREED 18: ACROBAT

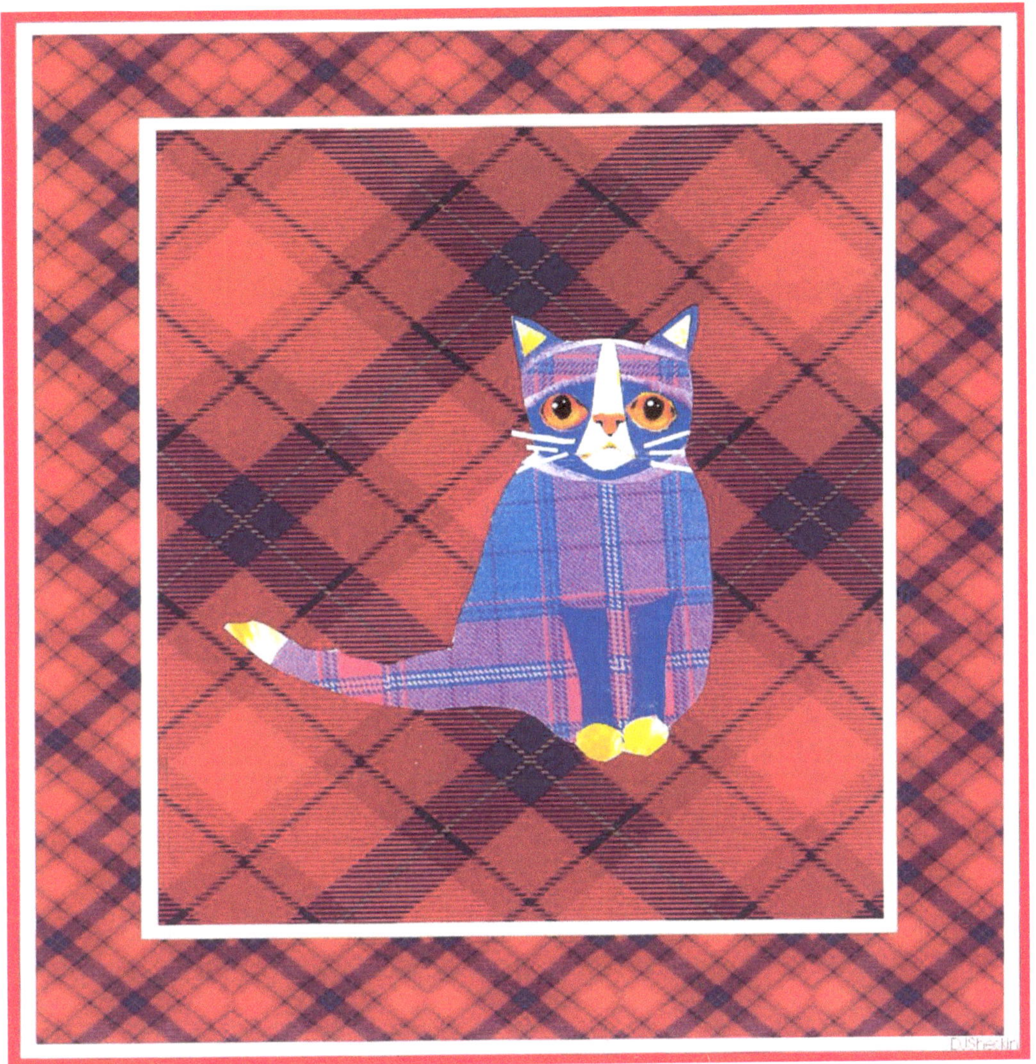

Breed 18: **Acrobat**
Best of Breed: *Tumbler*

The petite *Acrobat* is so named because of its incredible athletic ability. Possessing the climbing and jumping skills of tree monkeys, this brilliantly colored feline is often found in circuses where it is trained to perform complicated routines on apparatus such as high wires and trapeze. Originally a feral breed indigenous to the East Indies, it is now a favorite among cat owners. When kept as a pet it requires an environment that allows it regular and vigorous exercise. Difficult to breed in captivity, the *Acrobat* does best on a diet that consists of raspberries, cocoa beans, mangos, and baby bananas.

BREED 19: POPCORN

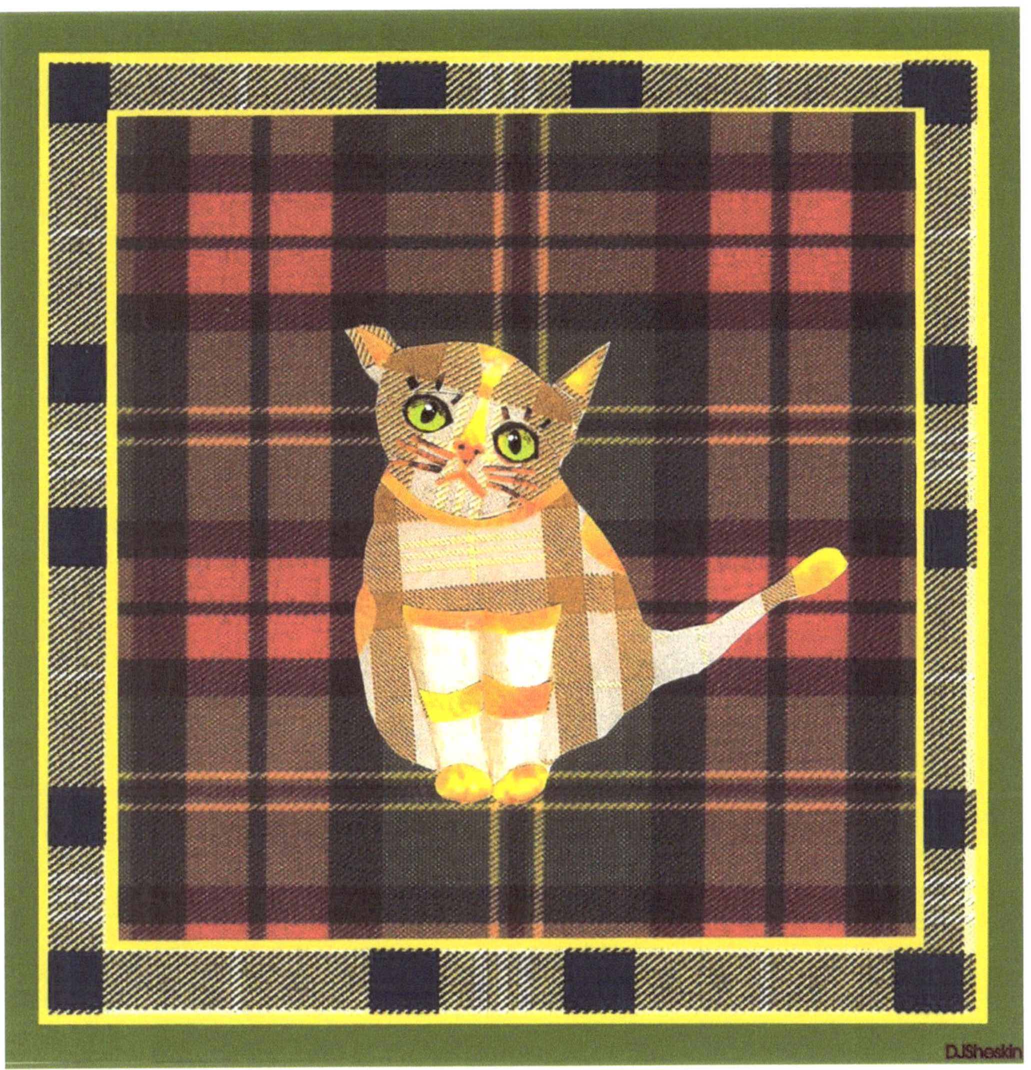

Breed 19: **Popcorn**
Best of Breed: *Hotshot*

Thought by some to be a distant relative of the *Peke-Face Persian*, the *Popcorn* is a small yet exceptionally strong cat who possesses a superb sense of balance. Characterized by piercing chartreuse eyes, bright red nose leather, and brilliant yellow paw pads, this energetic plaid breed make excellent companions for humans, and especially enjoys interacting with children. Because of their exceptional balance, *Popcorns* are perhaps more adept than any other breed at climbing and avoiding peril when situated high above the ground. Because this cat does not tolerate cold weather well, it should be kept indoors during the winter. *Popcorns* are happiest when allowed to eat a large variety of foods. Although individual animals have idiosyncratic preferences, among the most popular foods preferred by *Popcorns* are stuffed pepper, gazpacho, molasses, and scallions, and, of course, popcorn.

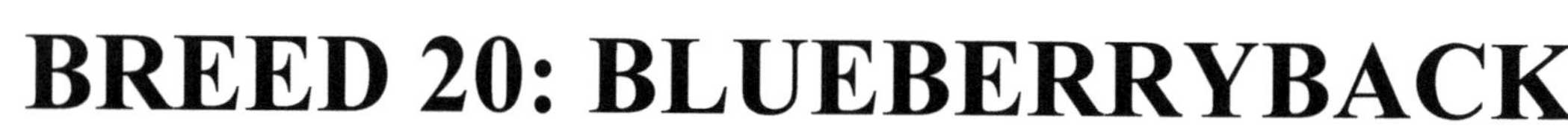

BREED 20: BLUEBERRYBACK

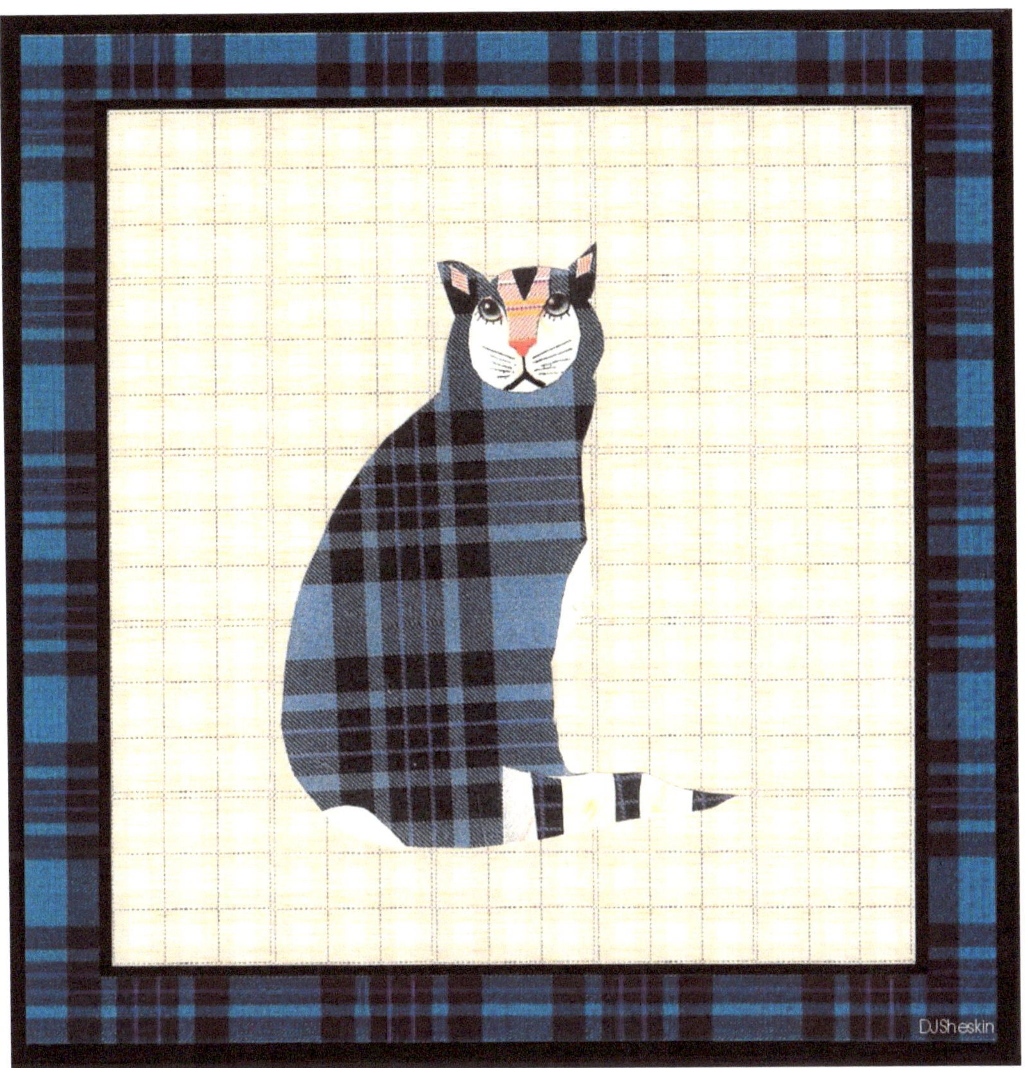

Breed 20: **Blueberryblack**
Best of Breed: *Shakespeare*

Extremely talkative, *Blueberryblacks* prefers human or feline companionship to solitude. These animals make excellent show cats because of their adaptability to new circumstances. Among the most intelligent of the plaid breeds, the *Blueberryblack* is adept at following commands and learning tricks. Kittens, generally two to four per litter, are surprisingly small at birth. They also lack their true coloring that doesn't develop until some time during the second year. The *Blueberryblack's* diet should include meat and giblets, although it will overeat when given the chance. Because of the latter food should only be given to this cat at prescribed times.

BREED 21: WATERMELON

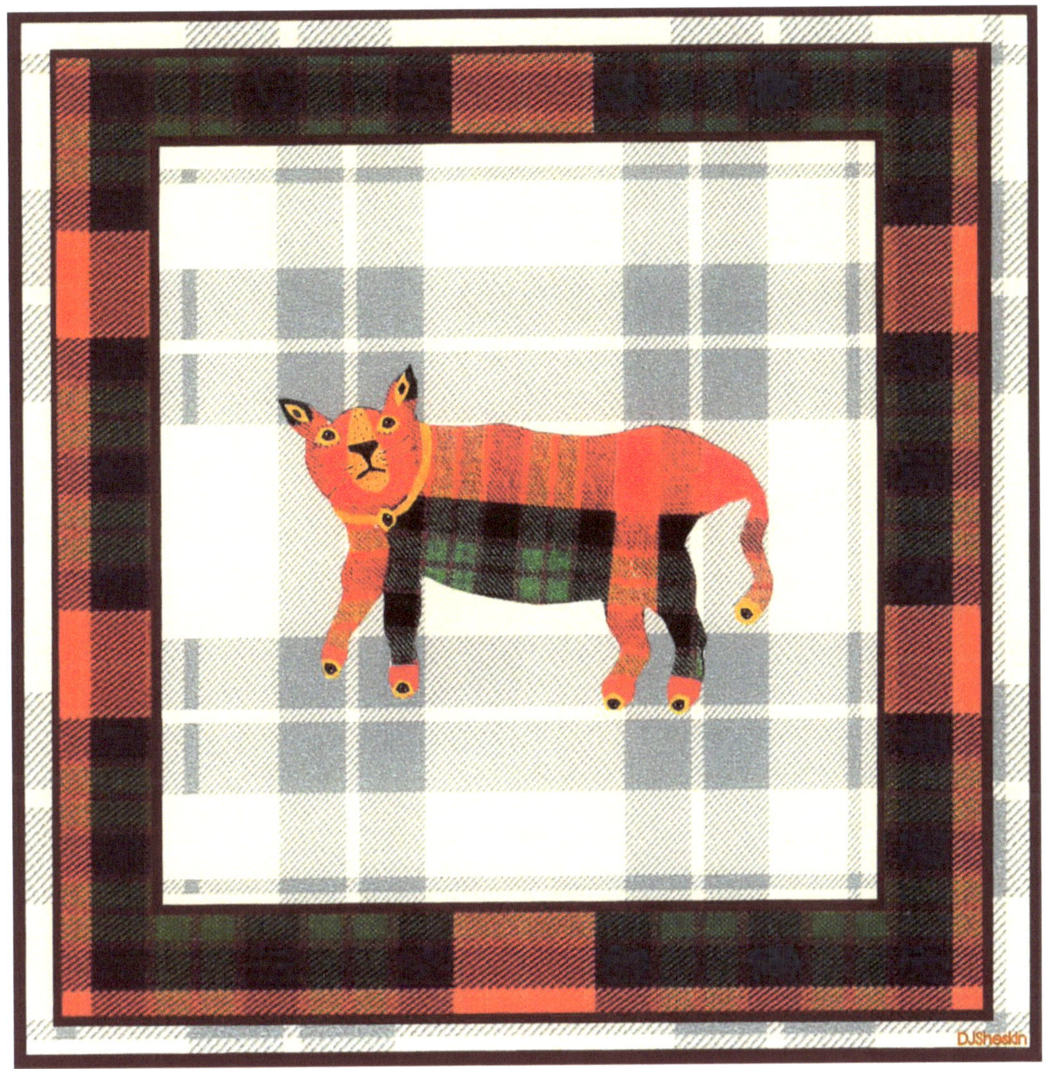

Breed 21: **Watermelon**
Best of Breed: *Pits*

The *Watermelon* was first identified by Vasco Nùnez de Balboa in the early 1500s living among the Indians in Guatemala. Easily domesticated, these playful little cats are noted for their extraordinary sensory acuity and endearing response to loving humans. *Watermelons* are noted for becoming agitated hours before the arrival of imminent dangers such as earthquakes and ferocious weather. Because the Indians reputedly told Balboa that changes in the behavior of these cats often foretold the approach of an attacking enemy, it is now not unusual for *Watermelons* to accompany armies into battle. The ideal show cat of this breed is characterized by the gold oval on the face and solid black nose leather. Although the upper part of the body is mostly orange and gold, the belly will almost always be dominated by green. These cats thrive on a diet that consists primarily of cornmeal, pistachio nuts, apricots, and insects. Because of their hypersensitivity to stimulation, *Watermelons* should be maintained in as calm an environment as possible.

BREED 22: ROYAL PLAID

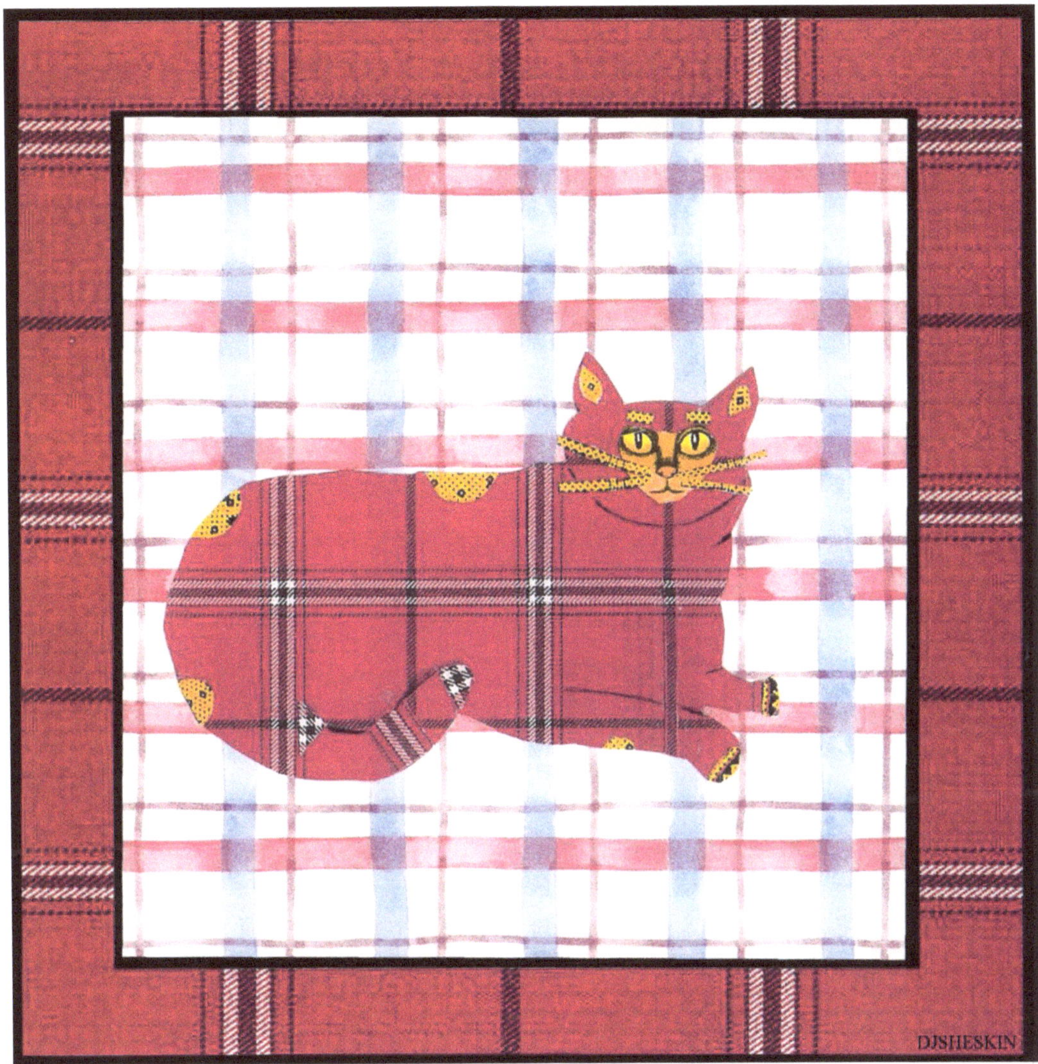

Breed 22: **Royal Plaid**
Best of Breed: *Biscuit*

Almost extinct in the 1960s due to irresponsible cross breeding, the official *Royal Plaid* breed was restored by a strict breeding program at the London Zoo. Although still extremely rare in captivity, most domesticated purebred *Royal Plaids* are the prized possessions of members of the British royal family. An extremely large cat, often weighing in excess of 40 pounds, the *Royal Plaid* is an unusually sensitive animal. Because of its keen sense of hearing, it has little tolerance for sudden or harsh noises. A typical litter yields only two kittens, each of which typically has plaid coats comprised of complementary colors. Both sexes are excellent feline parents. The preferred diet of the *Royal Plaid* is shellfish, salt pork, mutton, and maraschino cherries.

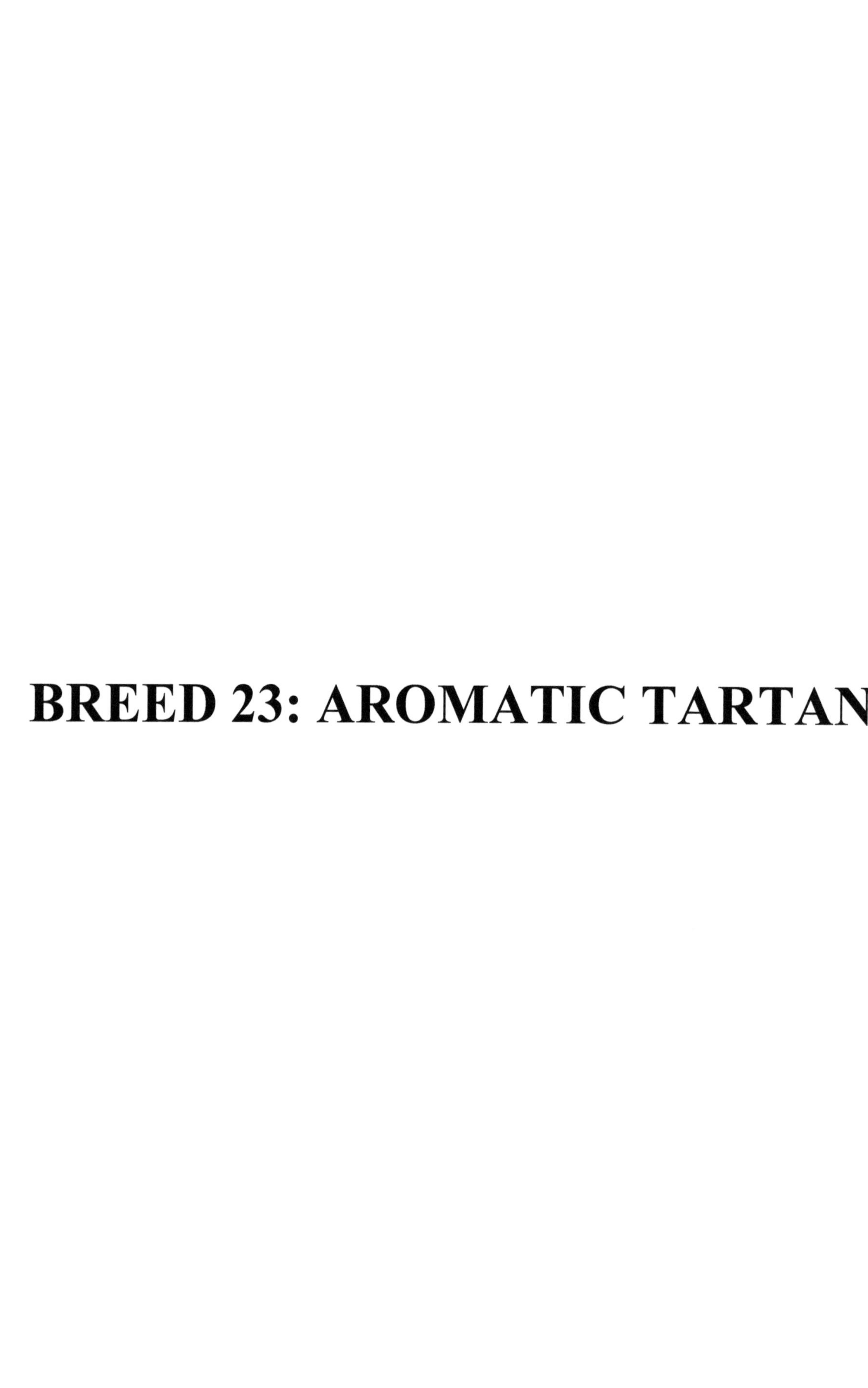

BREED 23: AROMATIC TARTAN

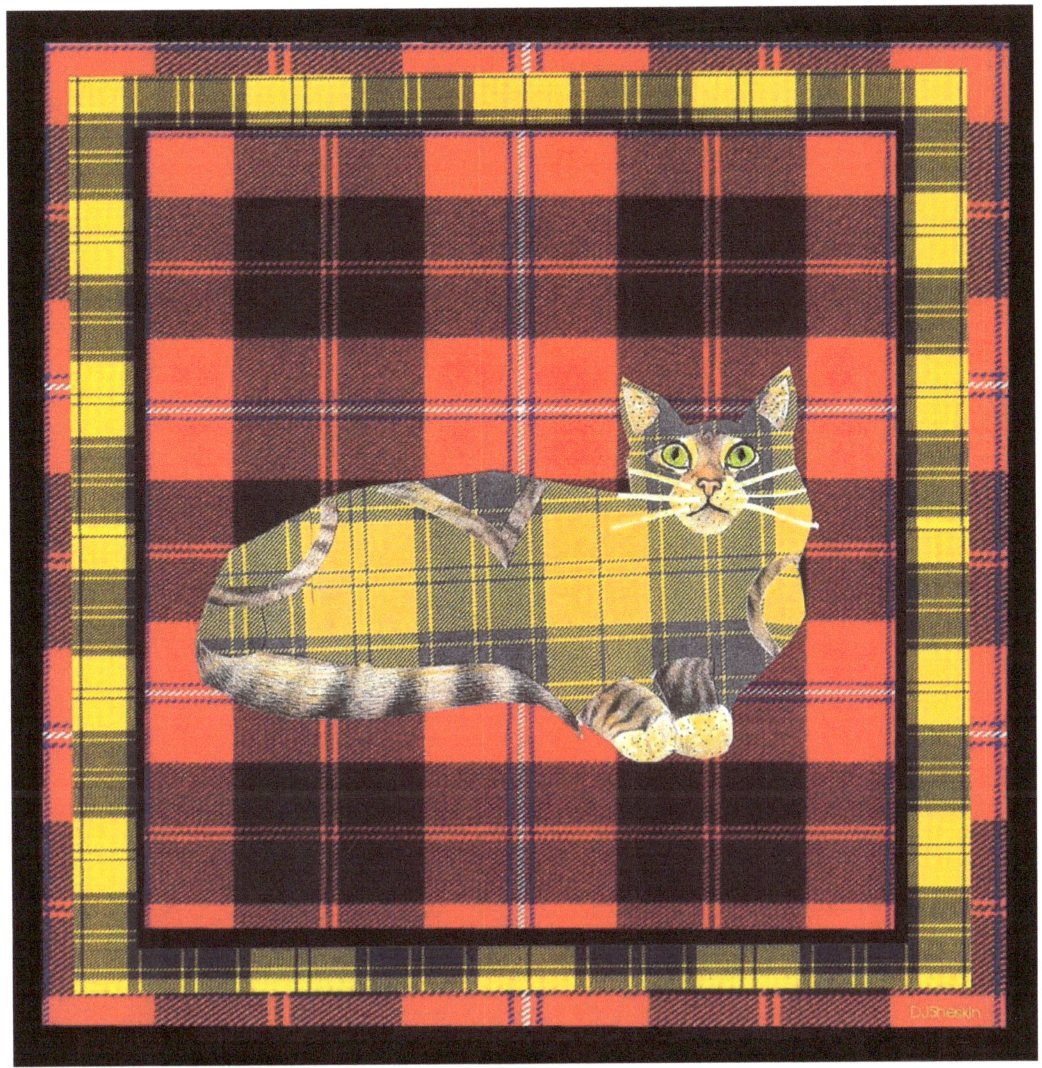

Breed 23: **Aromatic Tartan**
Best of Breed: *Brandy*

The *Aromatic Tartan* is among the most popular of the aromatic plaid breeds — the latter representing breeds whose secretions are characterized by a floral or fruity scent. Humans who have inhaled the secretions of the *Aromatic Tartan* typically describe its effect as both intoxicating and soothing. Sedentary by nature, these cats prefer nothing more than to sleep on top of their owner or sit in her lap for a prolonged period of time. A meticulous groomer, these cats are known for their handsome, fine textured, silky coat. The fruitiness of the breed's scent is best maintained on a balanced diet of meat, fish, and fowl. However, breeders have found that the addition of apricots and pears to the diet can help accentuate the natural odor of the *Aromatic Tartan*.

BREED 24: SVENGALI

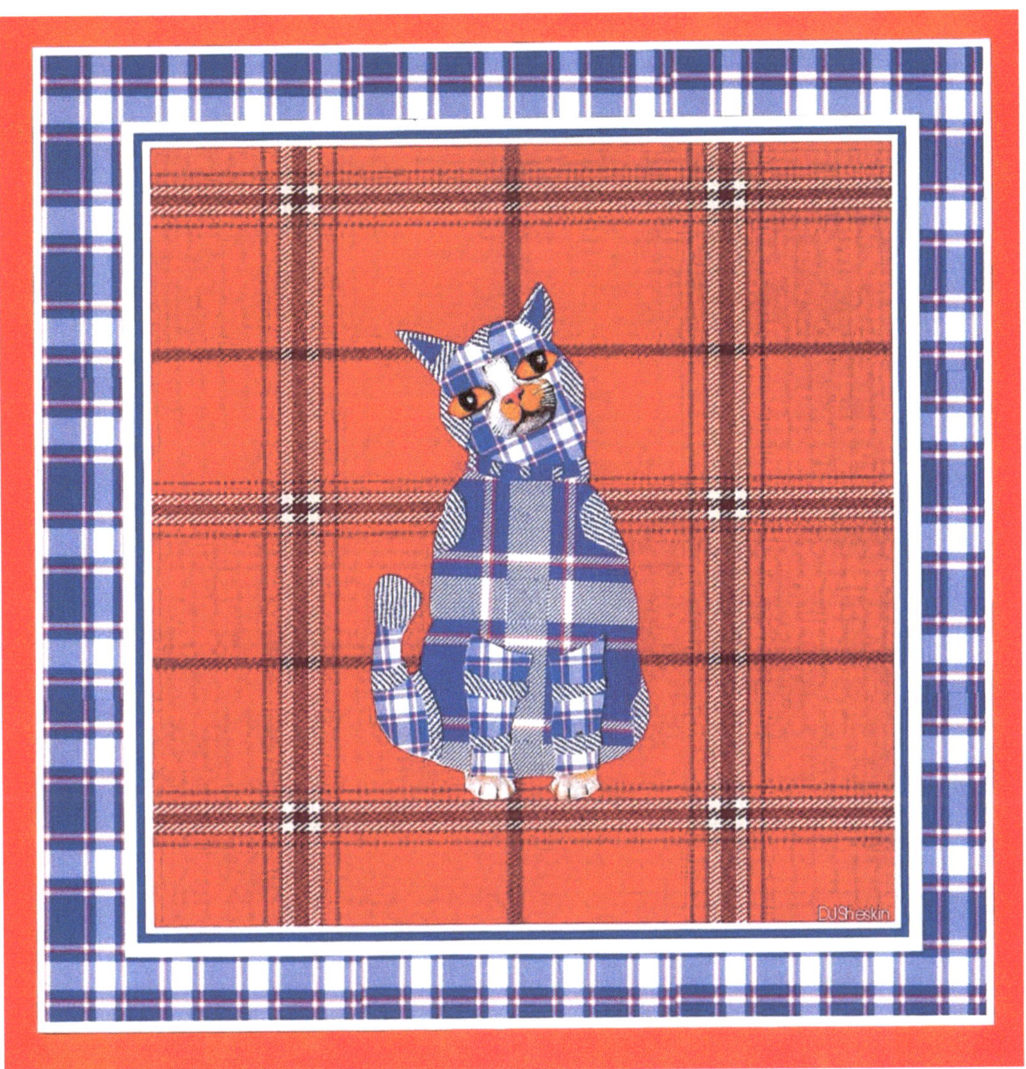

Breed 24: **Svengali**
Best of Breed: *Mesmer*

Known to incline its head and look into the eyes of its human companions for prolonged periods of time, legend has it that by returning the *Svengali's* stare a person will be transported into a state of total relaxation. Indeed, in certain parts of the world, this breed is often recommended by physicians as a remedy for dealing with stress and anxiety. An expensive cat, the *Svengali* is sought after by both amateur and professional cat lovers. Without question, it is numbered among the most intelligent of the feline breeds. Its solid, muscular body is covered with dense fur that sheds infrequently. Females usually produce litters of three or fewer kittens. *Svengali* are unique among felines in that they subsist almost exclusively on a diet of medicinal plants and preparations such as foxglove, syrup of ipecac, quinine, and belladonna.

BREED 25: CHAMPAGNE

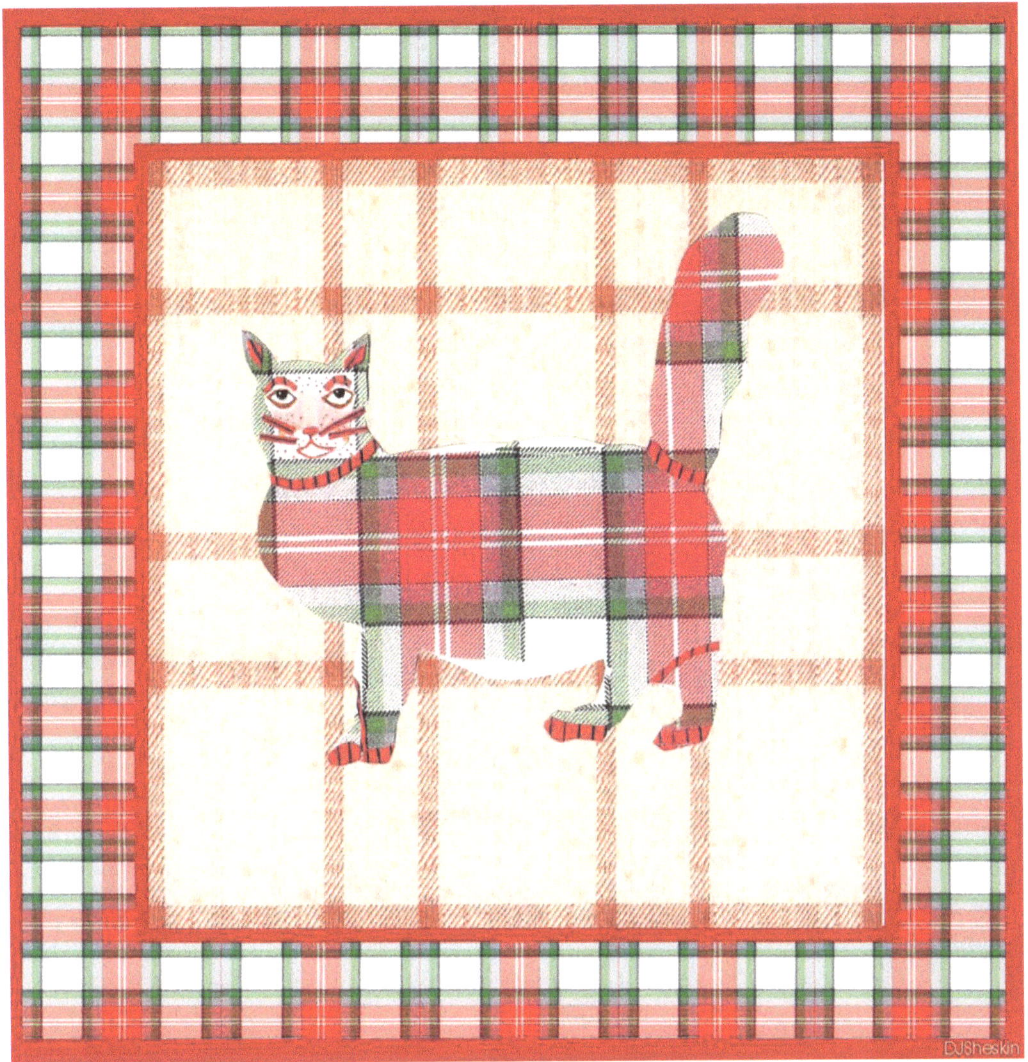

Breed 25: **Champagne**
Best of Breed: *Paris*

This unique French breed was produced through the accidental crossing of pedigreed and nonpedigreed plaids of mixed coloration biased toward the upper end of the spectrum. The fur of the *Champagne* is short and dense. The body is stocky and powerful with muscular legs, and a large bushy tail. Loving and even tempered, these cats make excellent companions who are tolerant of children and other cats. Breeding is a problem in that one quarter of the kittens are born tailless, and mating of two tailless cats often results in malformed animals who die before birth or soon after. The preferred diet of the *Champagne* is French cuisine, most notably, escargot, paté, truffles, foie gras, and, of course, their favorite beverage is champagne

BREED 26: PERFUME

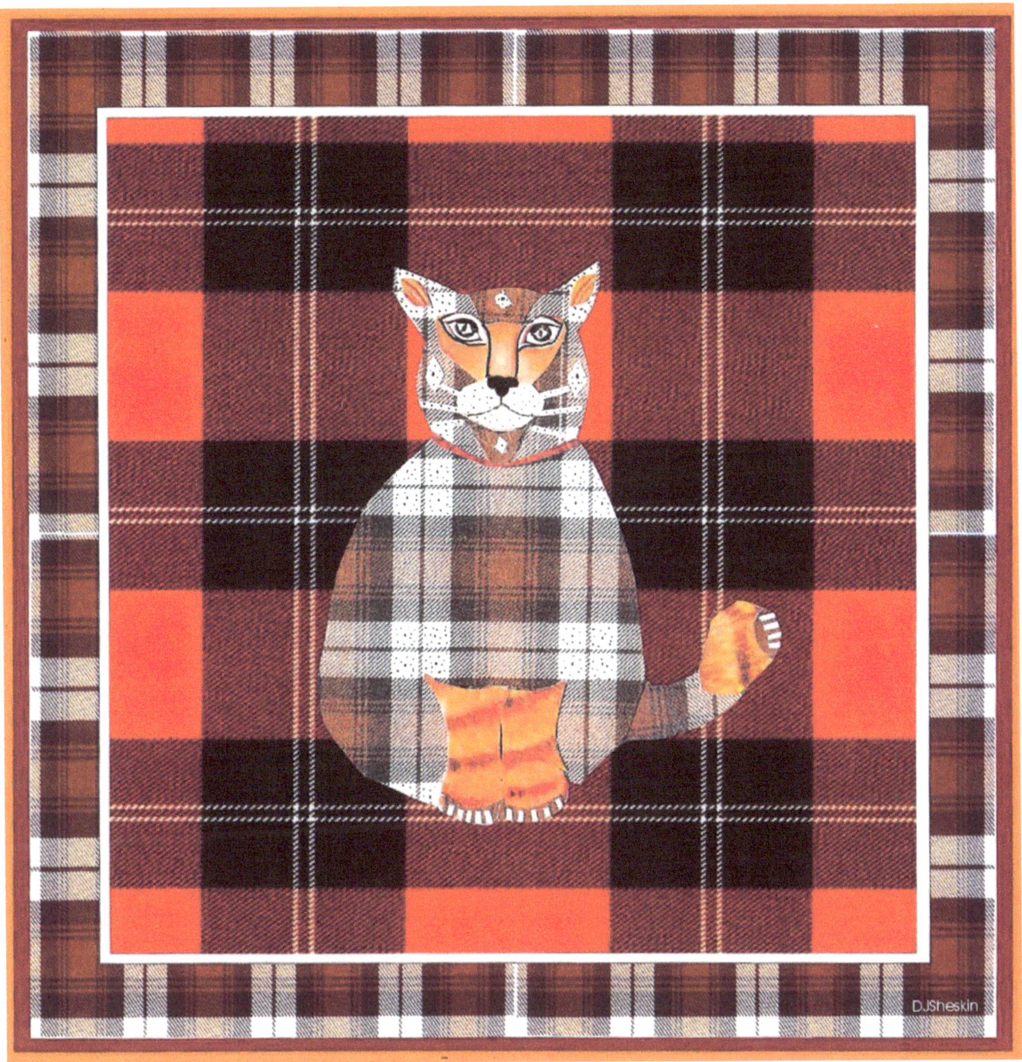

Breed 26: **Perfume**
Best of Breed: *Marmalade*

Known for the fruity scent it secretes while hunting, the *Perfume* is a breed that was first found in the jungles of Zanzibar. The *Perfume's* secretions appears to have a hypnotic effect on its prey, thus allowing it to attack a victim without encountering any resistance. Happiest living in the outdoors, this plaid breed has proven to be among the most difficult to domesticate. Temperamentally it is aloof and independent, and does best living unencumbered in an outdoors tropical environment. The few members of the breed that have been domesticated thrive best on a high protein diet rich in organ meats.

BREED 27: VELVET

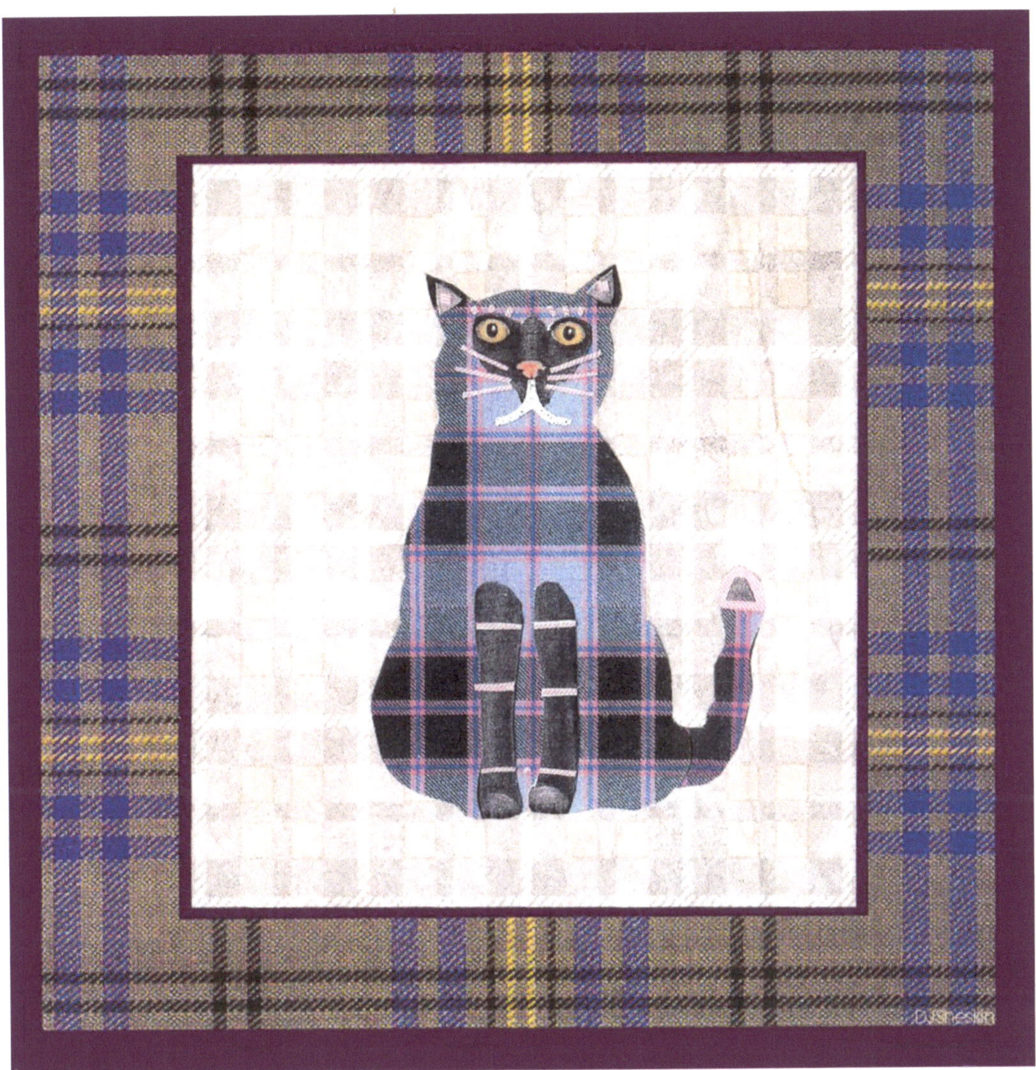

Breed 27: **Velvet**
Best of Breed: *Decadence*

This cat is named for its smooth, beautiful coat which has the feel of velvet. Aside from its lavender-tinted coat, an ideal *Velvet* has golden-colored eyes and bright red nose leather. When employed as a show cat, to enhance the animal's coat it should be bathed with an oatmeal based shampoo about a week prior to the show. Grooming with a silk handkerchief approximately eight hours before the show will maximize the sheen of the *Velvet's* coat. Temperamentally, *Velvets* are mellow, affectionate animals who enjoy being stroked a great deal. Although these cats are avid sunbathers, owners who show their cats should minimize the latter since it can result in fading of an animal's coloring. Although *Velvets* will eat a large variety of food, they especially enjoy treats such as buttermilk, whipped cream, and fruit frappés.

BREED 28: WARRIOR

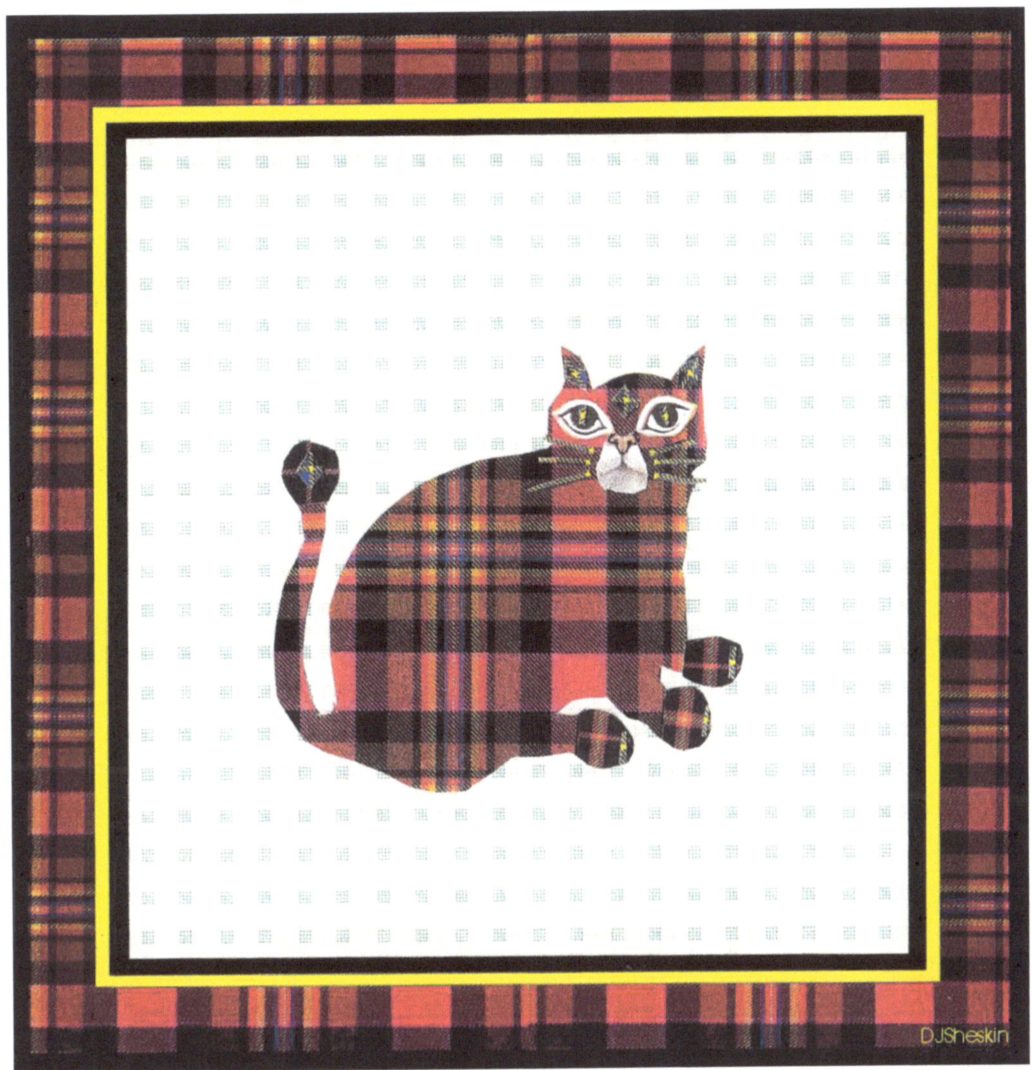

Breed 28: **Warrior**
Best of Breed: *Cha-Cha*

These compact, muscular cats come from Panama where the males of the breed are reputed to be great fighters yet, at the same time, excellent fathers who are devoted to the queen and their kittens. The *Warrior* is so named because of the complex dance both the male and female engage in before initiating mating. The fur of this breed is extremely fine and has a sheen that gives it an almost metallic look. The *Warrior* tends to be high strung and is extremely reactive to loud noise and other unexpected stimulation. Because of this it should be kept in a tranquil environment. The preferred diet of these cats is bananas, rhubarb, and roasted fowl, preferably squab or pheasant.

BREED 29: SPHINX

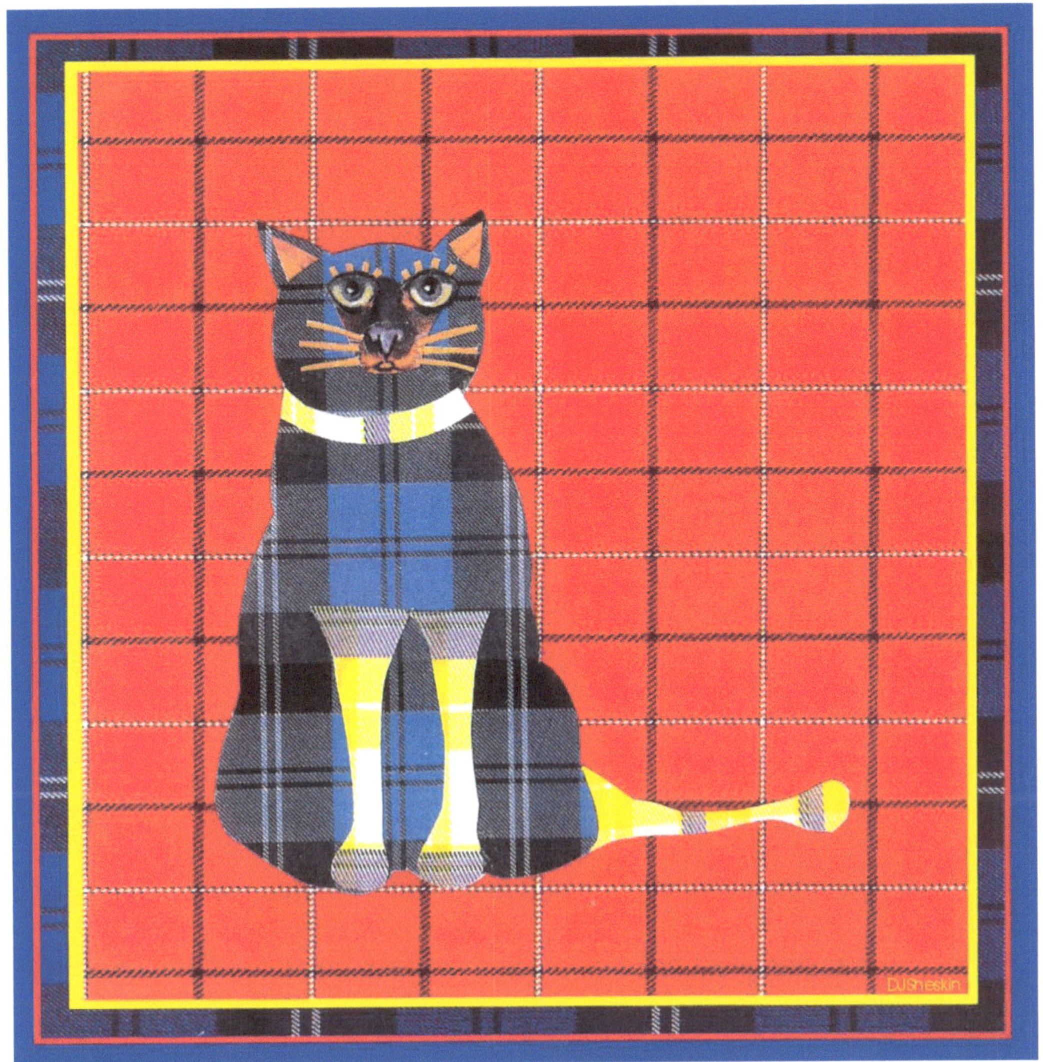

Breed 29: **Sphinx**
Best of Breed: *Caesar*

Not to be confused with the lean, hairless *Sphynx*, the *Sphinx* is a breed that is reputed to have been captured by the Romans while fighting in Egypt about 200 BC. Legend has is from that point on Roman warriors had these powerful, bow-legged cats accompany them on subsequent campaigns. The *Sphinx* is a tough, hardy animal that adapts well to virtually any kind of climate. Difficult to domesticate, these handsome, intelligent cats are exclusively carnivorous subsisting on small mammals, lizards, and snakes. The fur of these magnificent animals has an almost leather-like feel. Females are more amenable to domestication than males. The domesticated *Sphinx* should be fed meat and poultry dishes, but owners should not expect to get a great deal of affection from these cats. The few *Sphinx* that have been entered in cat shows have won numerous ribbons.

BREED 30: CASANOVA

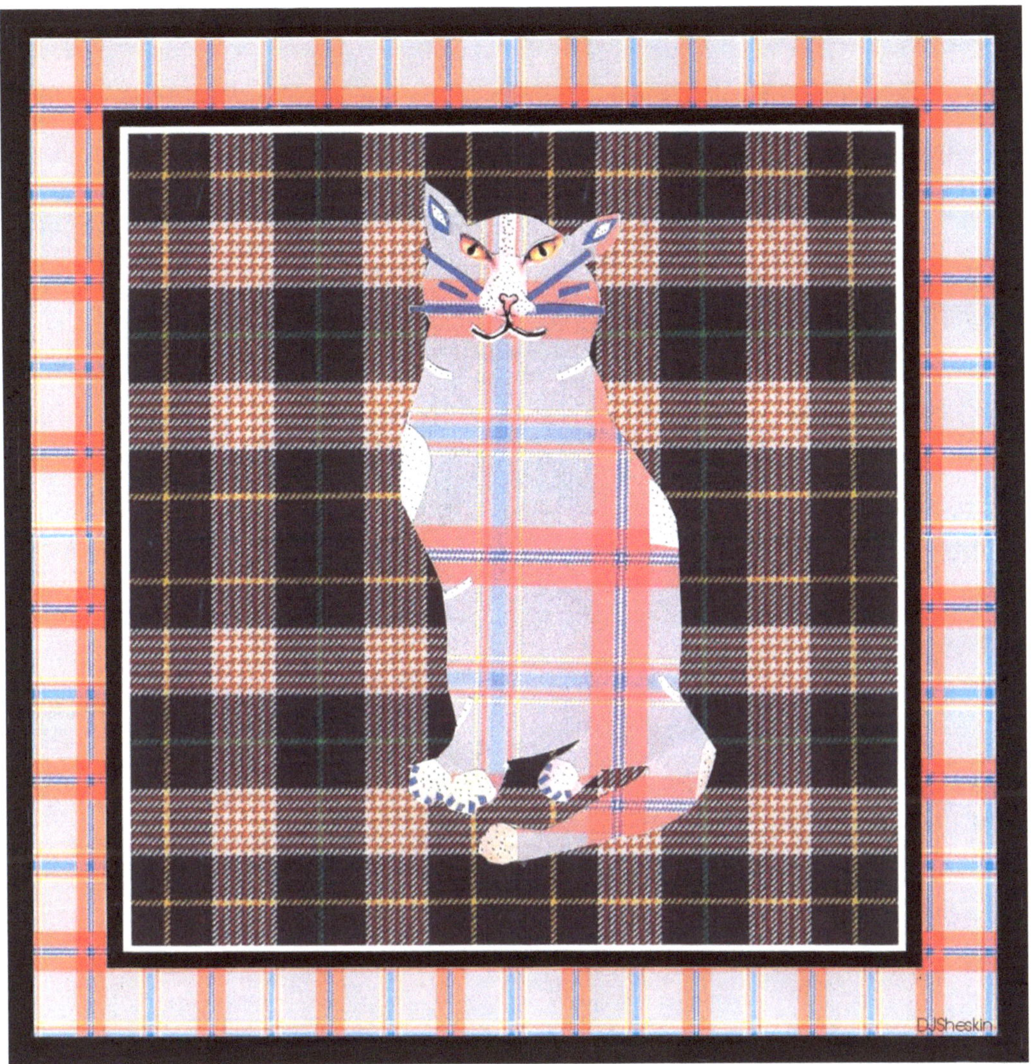

Breed 30: **Casanova**
Best of Breed: *Lord Byron*

The name *Casanova* is only employed for the male of this breed who, like his namesake, is reputed for his prowess with females. Females represent one of a number of cats that fall within the plaid breeds who do not have a plaid coat. Such animals are referred to *Neutral Plaids*. The coat of the female, who is unusually docile and even tempered, is solid grey. The *Casanova*, on the other hand, is both persistent and assertive, as well as being extremely resourceful in gaining access to females in heat. *Casanovas* exhibit little or no allegiance toward their kittens or the numerous queens they impregnate. The fur of these cats is thick and bristly, and their jaws and forequarters are extremely powerful. Although the female is easily domesticated, the *Casanova* does not adapt well to living indoors. When living outdoors he subsists on small mammals, insects, and snakes.

BREED 31: MAGNOLIA

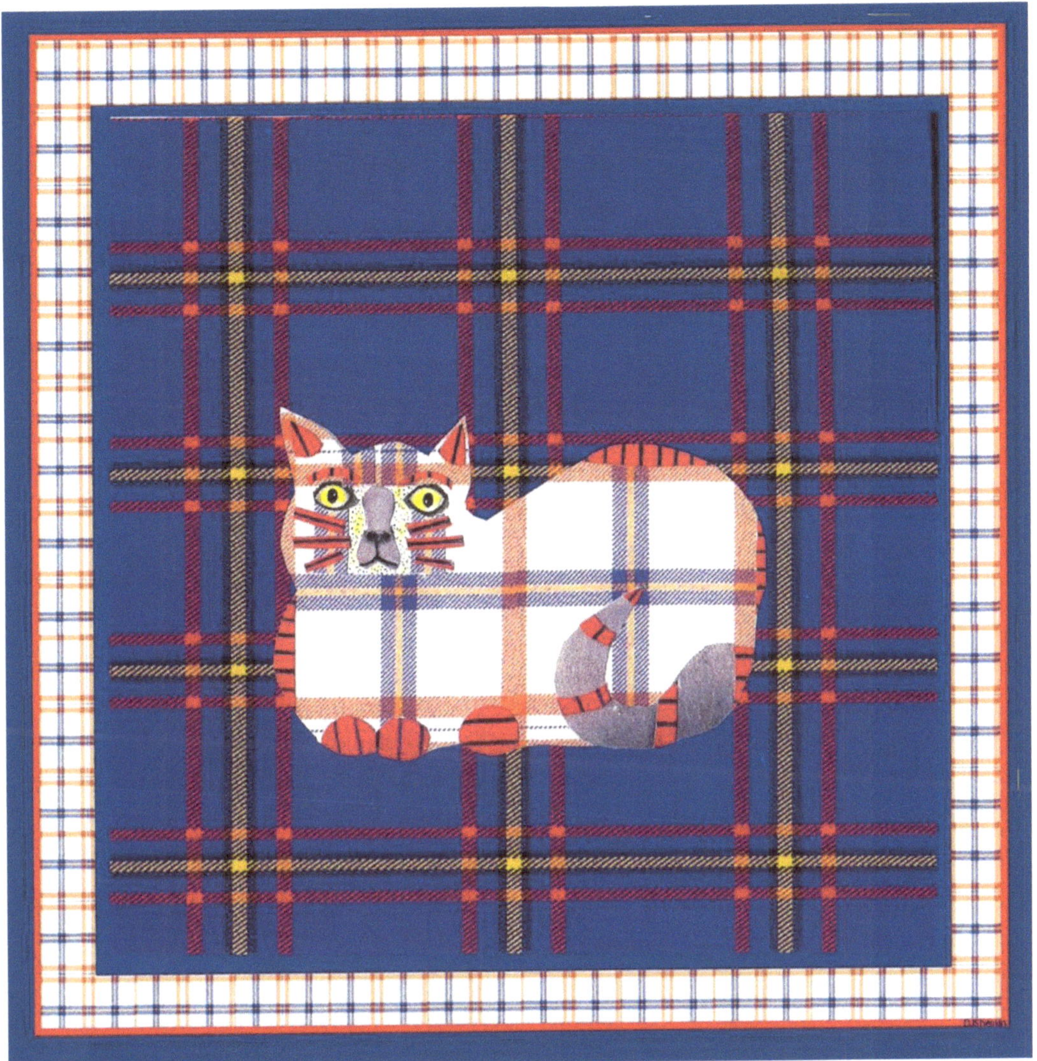

Breed 31: **Magnolia**
Best of Breed: *Gladys*

The *Magnolia* is the result of selective cross breeding among several breeds of plaids in which spontaneous mutations had occurred. The delicate movements and fragile-looking appearance of this cat are misleading. *Magnolia* are strong, muscular, and clever, and are able to use their paws to gain access to difficult areas as well as to defend themselves against more formidable looking adversaries. When living indoors, daily brushing of the *Magnolia* is recommended as is periodic bathing. The diet of this breed should be restricted to Mediterranean flowering plants such as anemone, snapdragon, clustered bellflower, and horned poppy. *Magnolia* will refuse to eat red meat and are highly allergic to shellfish.

BREED 32: WHIRLIGIG

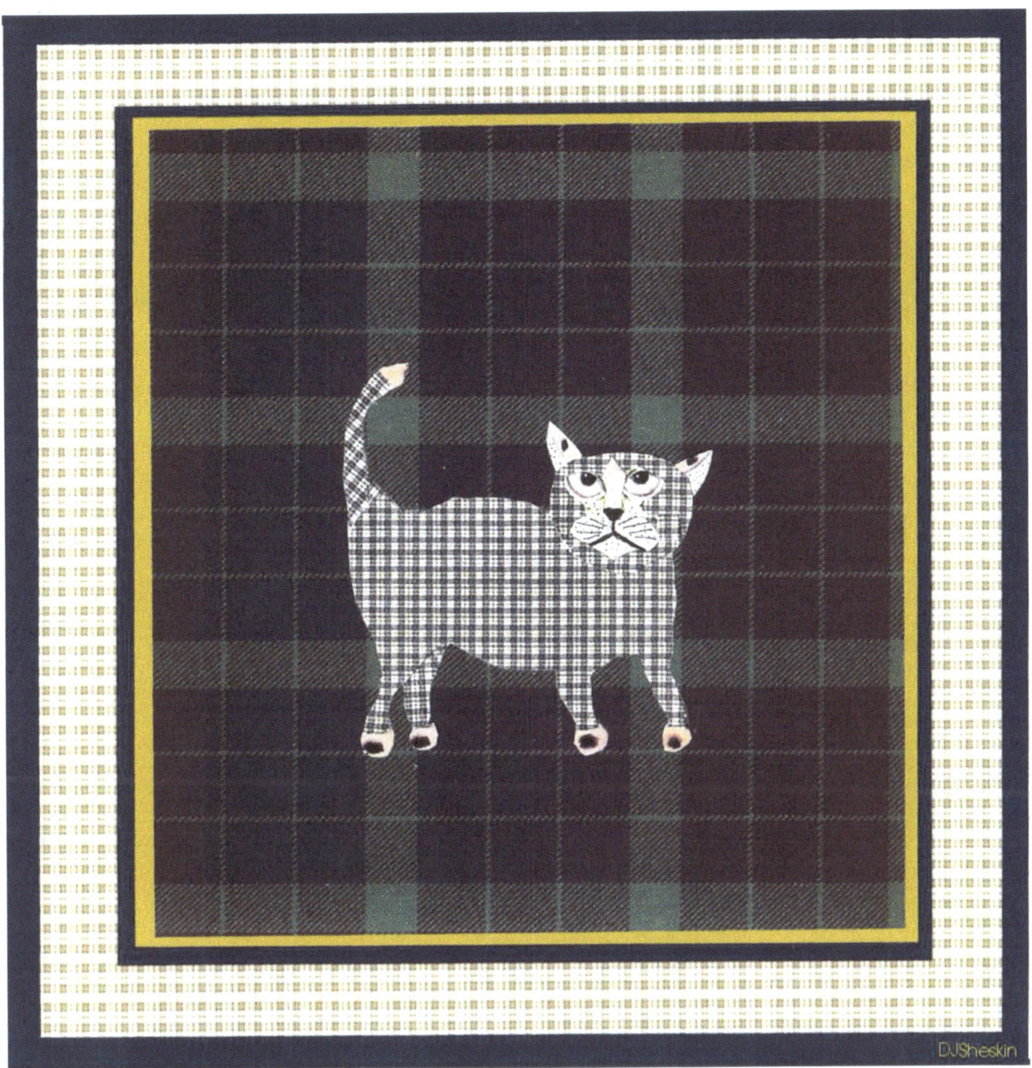

Breed 32: **Whirligig**
Best of Breed: *Topspin*

Known for its predilection to spin its body around as if it were a top, this playful little cat is the ideal pet for a family with children. Affectionate and gregarious, as well as having a seemingly endless amount of energy, the *Whirligig* is known to entertain its owners from morning through the evening. Its checkered coat and sad looking face inevitably gain both the attention and affection of strangers who come into contact with it. This is a hardy breed that typically lives to a relatively old age, often more than twenty years. Although it eats just about anything you give it, the *Whirligig* is especially partial toward Chinese cuisine, most notably wonton soup, chicken chow mein, and egg rolls.

BREED 33: NEON

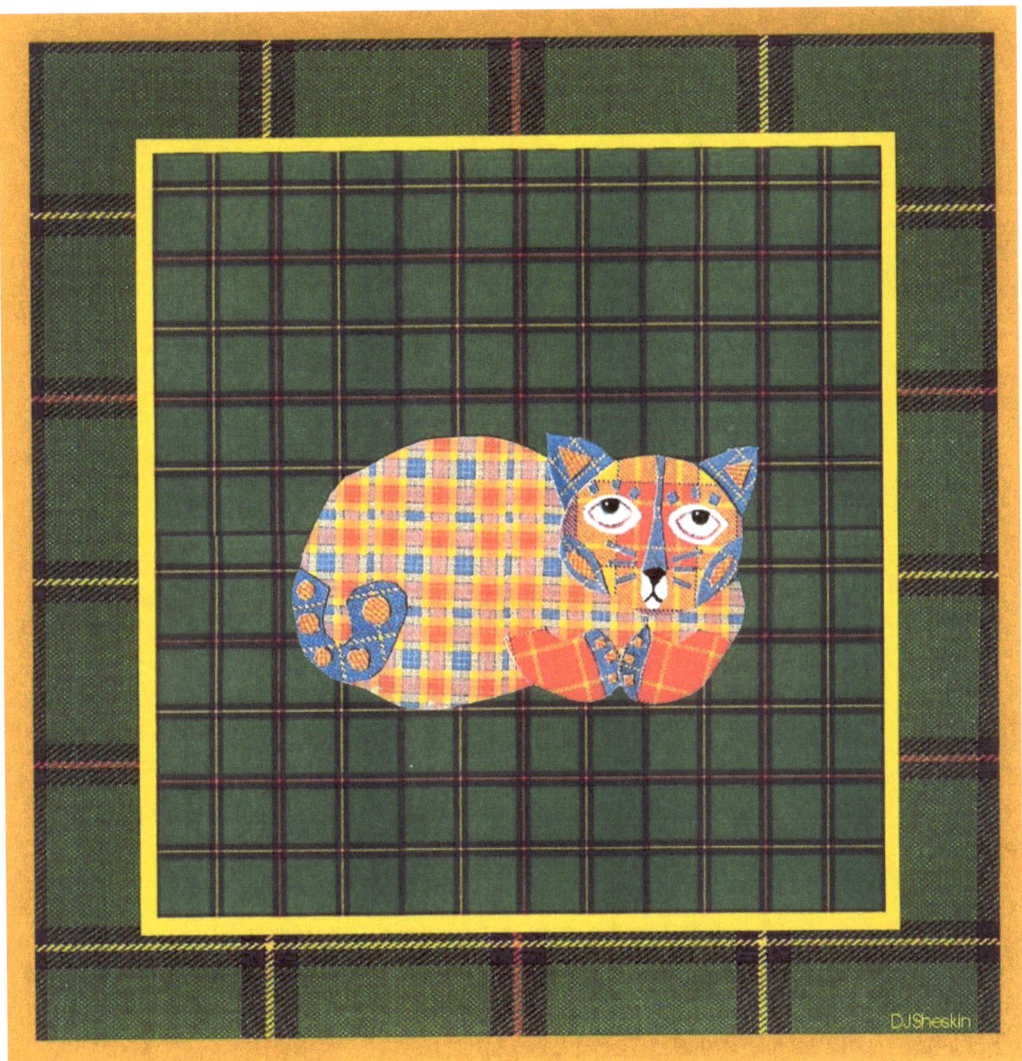

Breed 33: **Neon**
Best of Breed: *Halo*

The result of complicated cross breeding, this remarkable cat is best known for the fact that the orange elements in its coloring glow in the dark. An extremely sensual cat, the *Neon* loves to sunbathe and especially enjoys tummy rubs and being tickled behind the ears. This breed is free with its affection, generally returning what is given. Children often are its favorites. The kittens are generally much darker than their parents, gaining their true colors only at maturity. Favorite foods are red beets, turnips, asparagus, and salt water taffy (which is reputed to enhance the luminosity of its orange markings).

BREED 34: LUPINE

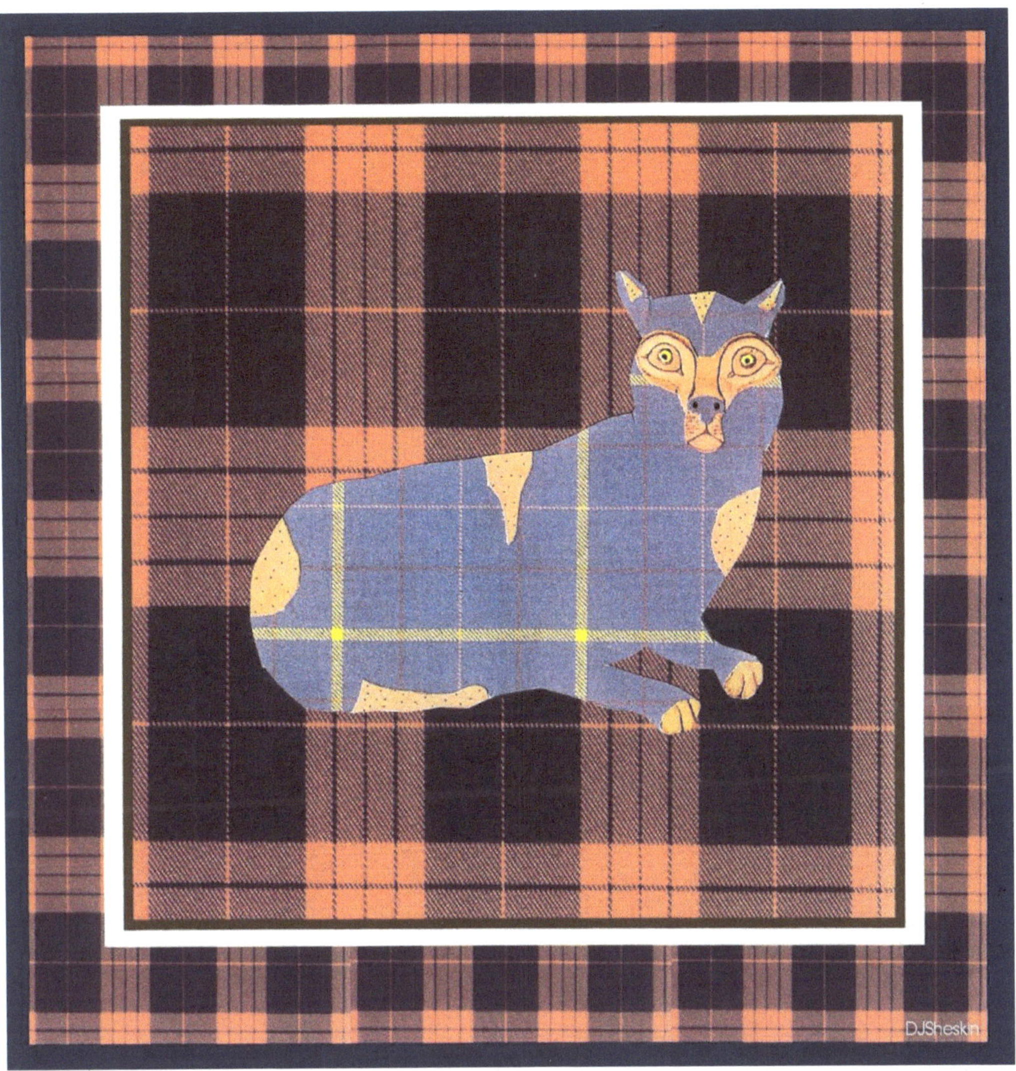

Breed 34: **Lupine**
Best of Breed: *Foxy*

A distant relative of the red fox, the *Lupine* is a recent product of genetic engineering. Ninety percent feline and 10% lupine, members of this breed are exceptional hunters. Cautious by nature, as well as being somewhat aggressive, the Foxy has proven difficult to completely domesticate. Yet in spite of the latter, it is prized as a working cat by farmers in the colder environs of North America and Europe. The breed hunts small mammals and birds, as well as being an excellent fisherman. Since the *Lupine* will not breed in captivity, those interested in breeding it must provide this cat with an appropriate outdoor environment. In spite of the difficulties associated with domesticating this breed, it is becomingly increasingly more common to see the *Lupine* numbered among those breeds displayed at cat shows.

BREED 35: LEPRECHAUN

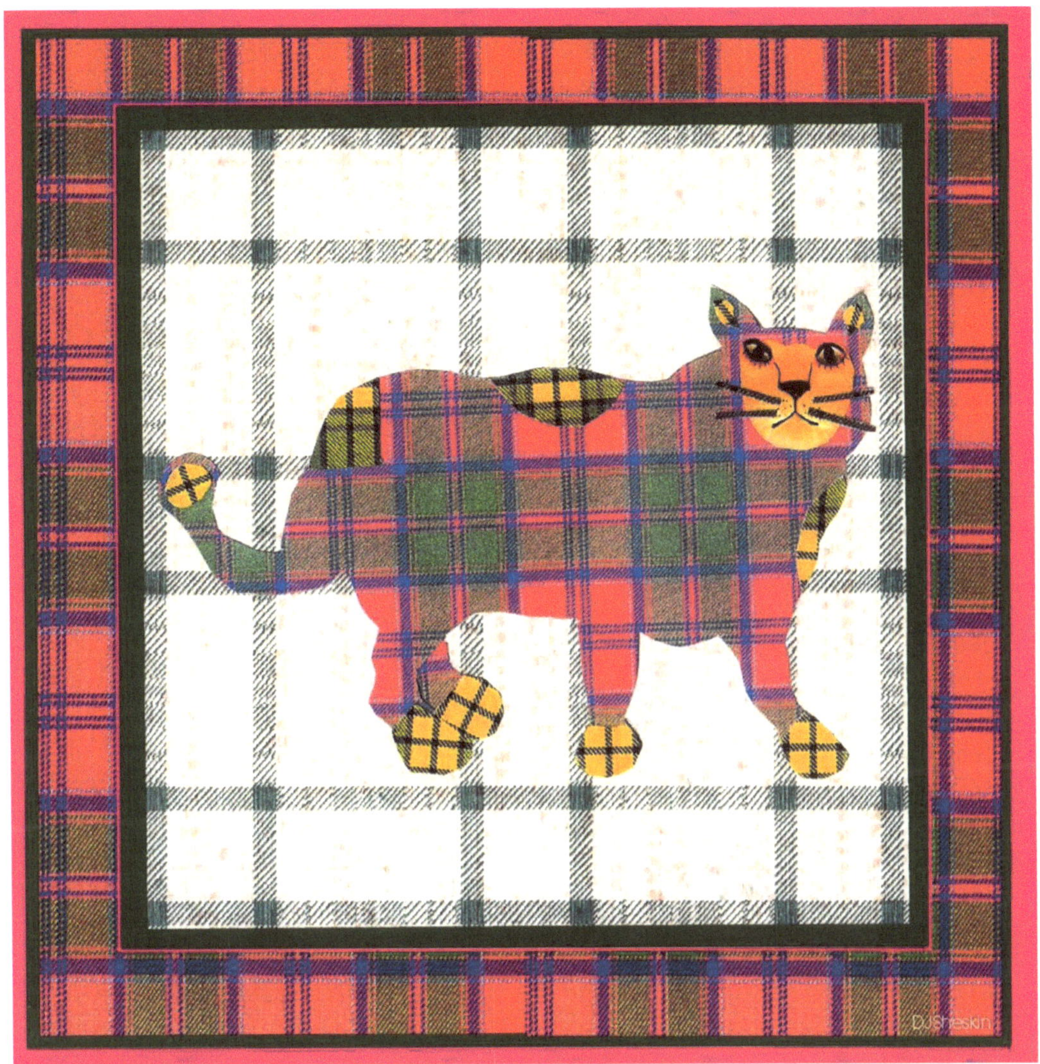

Breed 35: **Leprechaun**
Best of Breed: *Shamrock*

Domesticated in Ireland during the 1700s, this clever breed is best known for its aptitude and perseverance as a hunter. The *Leprechaun's* body is stocky and broad with extremely powerful legs. The fur, which is thick and dense, is characterized by an aroma that is best described as blend of peppermint and sandalwood. Because of the latter, humans enjoy holding this cat and burying one's nose in its sumptuous coat. These sociable creatures, who possess a melodious purr, make excellent pets and do best on a diet of Irish stew, boiled potatoes, and corn beef hash.

BREED 36: CYCLONE

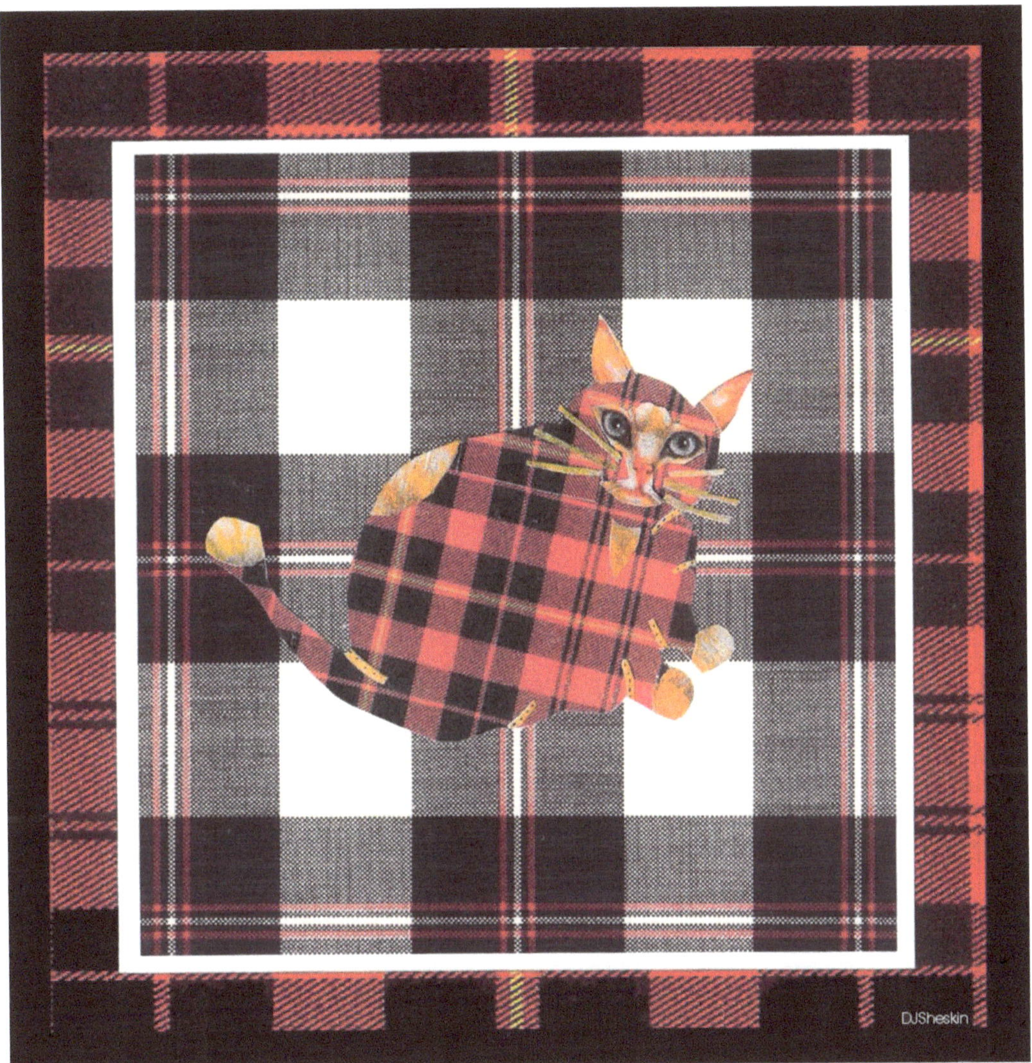

Breed 36: **Cyclone**
Best of Breed: *Jellyroll*

More than any other species the *Cyclone* needs an owner who will provide it with play and exercise. Without the latter these cats may become sullen and withdrawn. On the other hand, owners observe that a content *Cyclone* rarely stops purring. Because of its high level of energy this breed does best when it has periodic access to an outdoor environment. Kittens are born with solid red or black coloring, obtaining their plaid pattern sometime during their first and second year. Sustained exposure to sunlight, however, does facilitates the development of the stripes. This breed thrives on a diet that involves large portions of pureed fruits, custard, and jellyrolls.

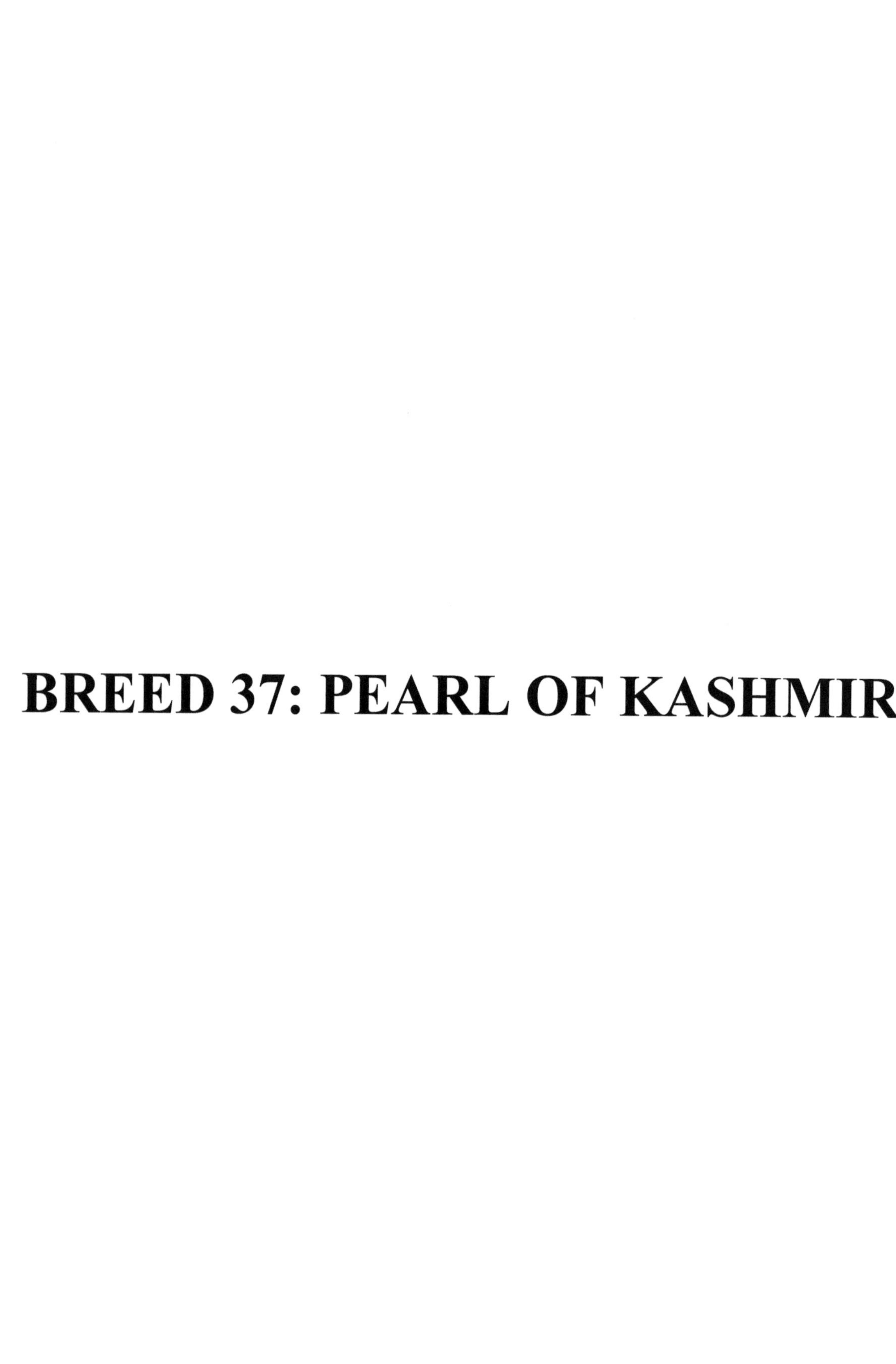

BREED 37: PEARL OF KASHMIR

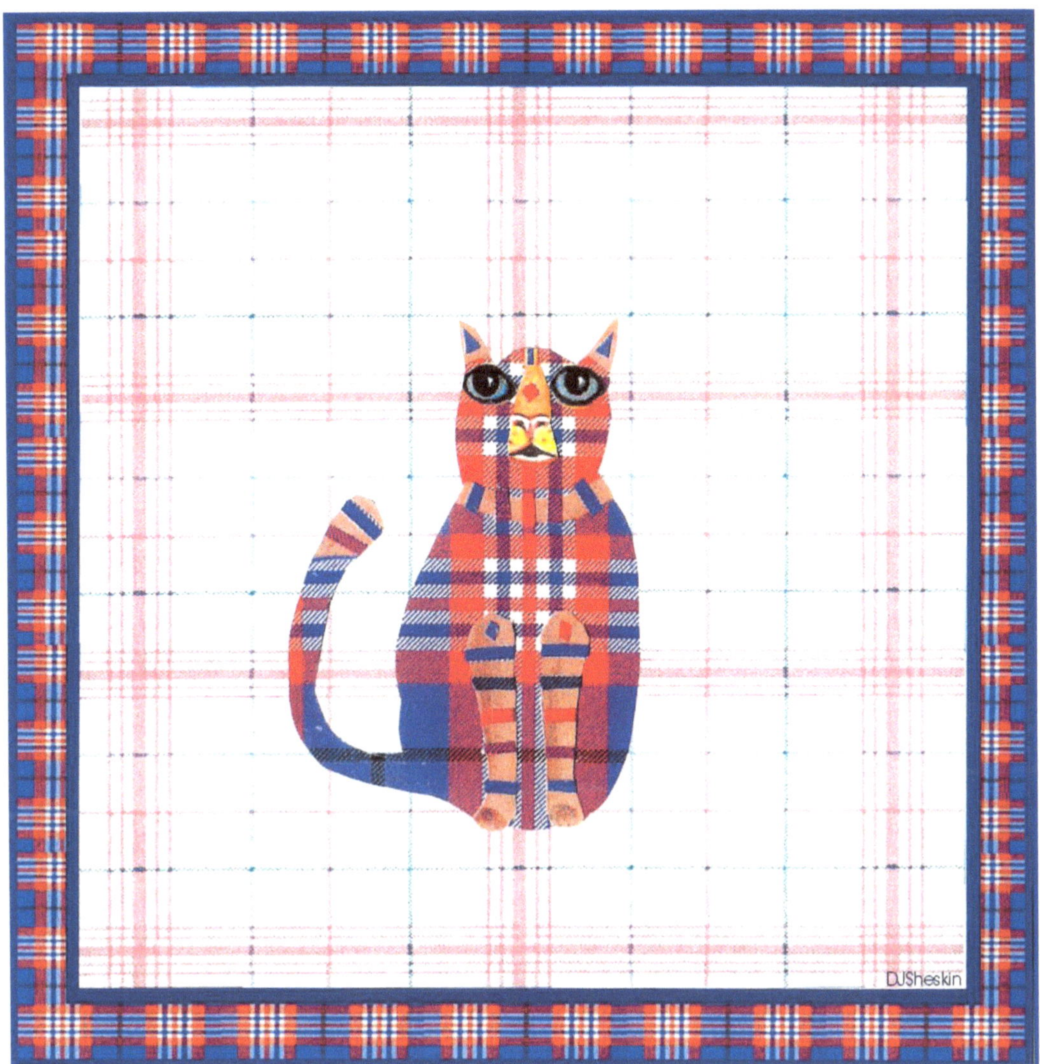

Breed 37: **Pearl of Kashmir**
Best of Breed: *Tutti-Fruitti*

The *Pearl of Kashmir* was first identified in the 1800s living in the mountains of Kashmir. Revered by the natives as sacred, some female members of the breed were semi-domesticated to live inside temples. Heavy and well-muscled, the *Pearl of Kashmir* is an adept hunter who is not naturally inclined to live with humans. Happiest when outdoors where it is free to roam and hunt for small mammals and lizards, these cats are extremely hearty and have been known to live as long as 35 years. To date no one has been successful in breeding the *Pearl of Kashmir* while in captivity. Litters of four to six kittens are born to parents who encourage their offspring to become independent at an early age.

BREED 38: SUGARCANE

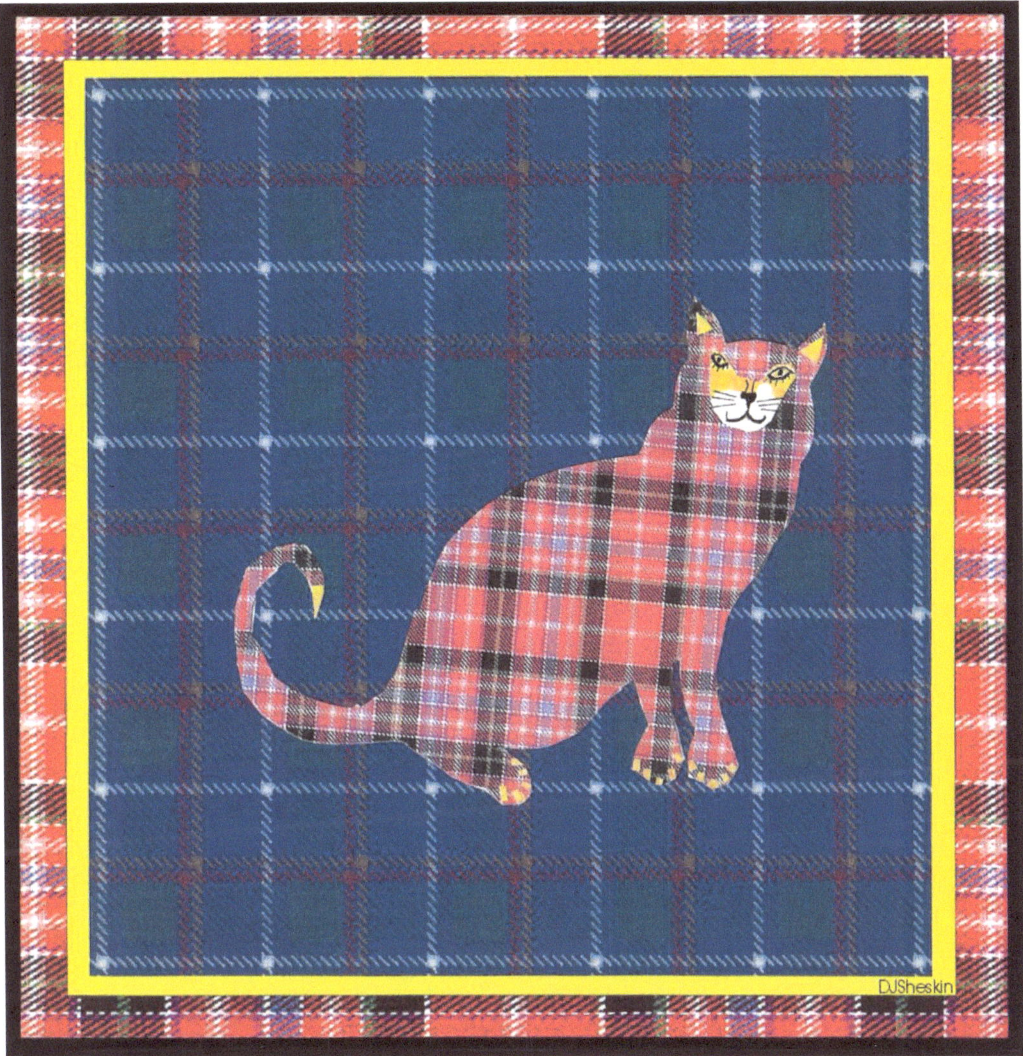

Breed 38: **Sugarcane**
Best of Breed: *Candy*

This brilliantly colored breed is noted for its sweet tooth, exhibiting a definite preference for chocolate morsels such as tootsie rolls, bon-bons, chocolate kisses and malt balls. *Sugarcanes* are gentle and placid and their disposition has been described by their owners as being as sweet as the expression on their face. Docile by nature, they prefer a soothing indoor environment in which they are comfortable and pampered. When *Sugarcanes* speak, their voice is soft and quiet, and speech is usually a sign that the cat wants some extra attention. Litters of five to seven kittens are born to conscientious parents who spend a considerable amount of time grooming and attending to their offspring.

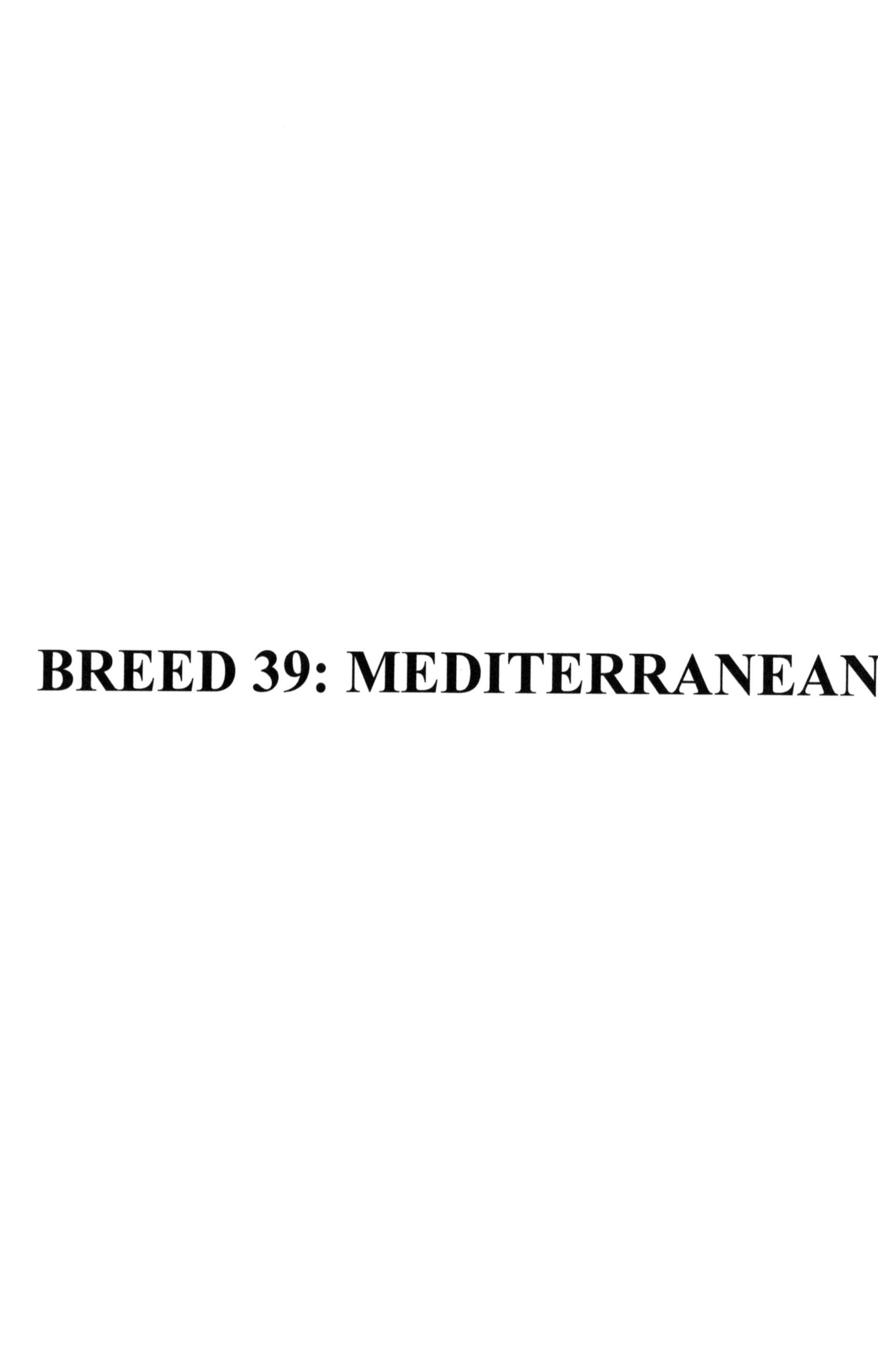

BREED 39: MEDITERRANEAN

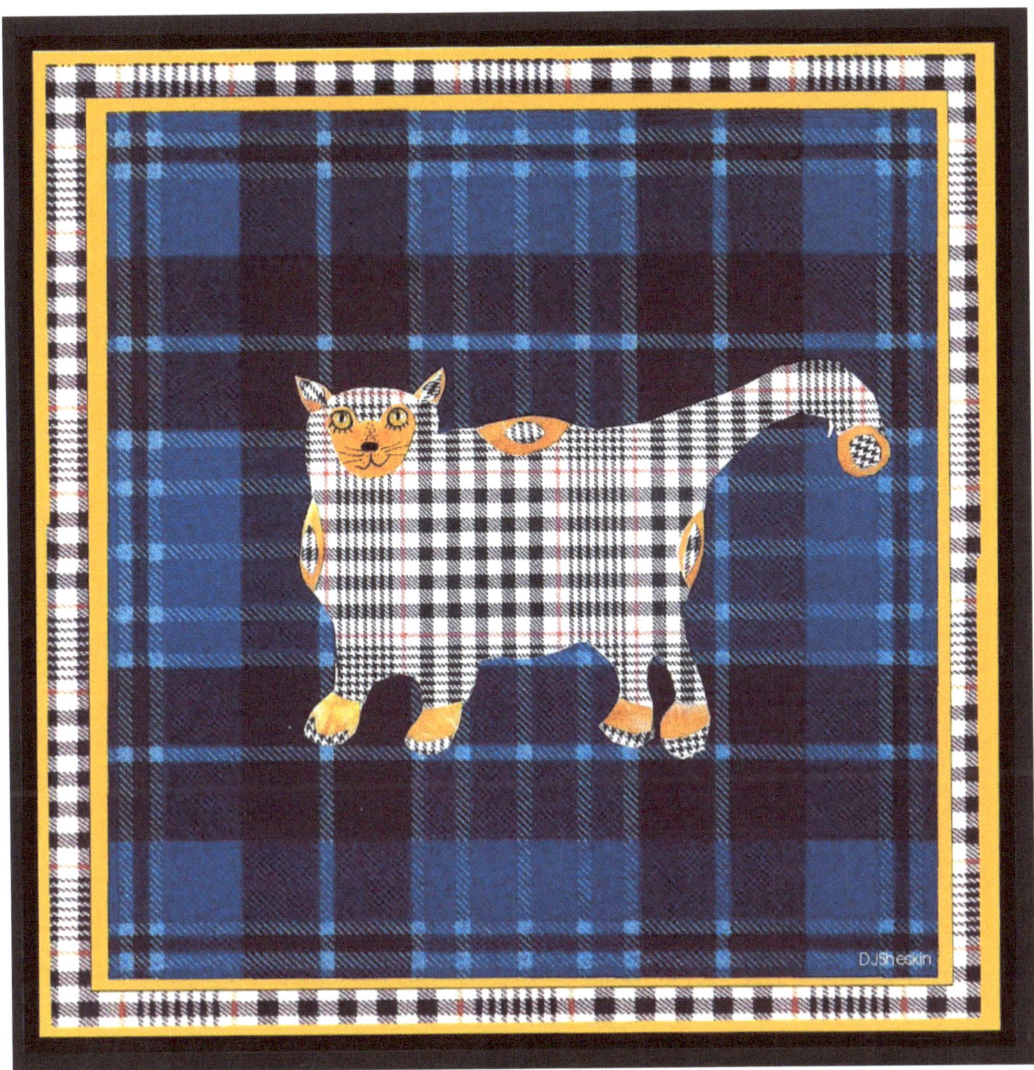

Breed 39: **Mediterranean**
Best of Breed: *Domino*

The exact history of this breed is unknown, with the earliest records locating it on the islands of Corsica and Sardinia. Scrupulously bred in catteries along the southwest coast of Italy, since the 1950s the *Mediterranean* has become a popular house pet throughout Italy and the Grecian Isles. A voracious eater, the *Mediterranean* must be watched carefully in order to avoid problems with obesity. Litters of six to eight kittens are born to attentive parents who spend a considerable amount of time playing with their offspring. The preferred cuisine of the *Mediterranean* is lasagna, meatballs and spaghetti, all varieties of pasta, and fried eggplant.

BREED 40: PEEKABOO

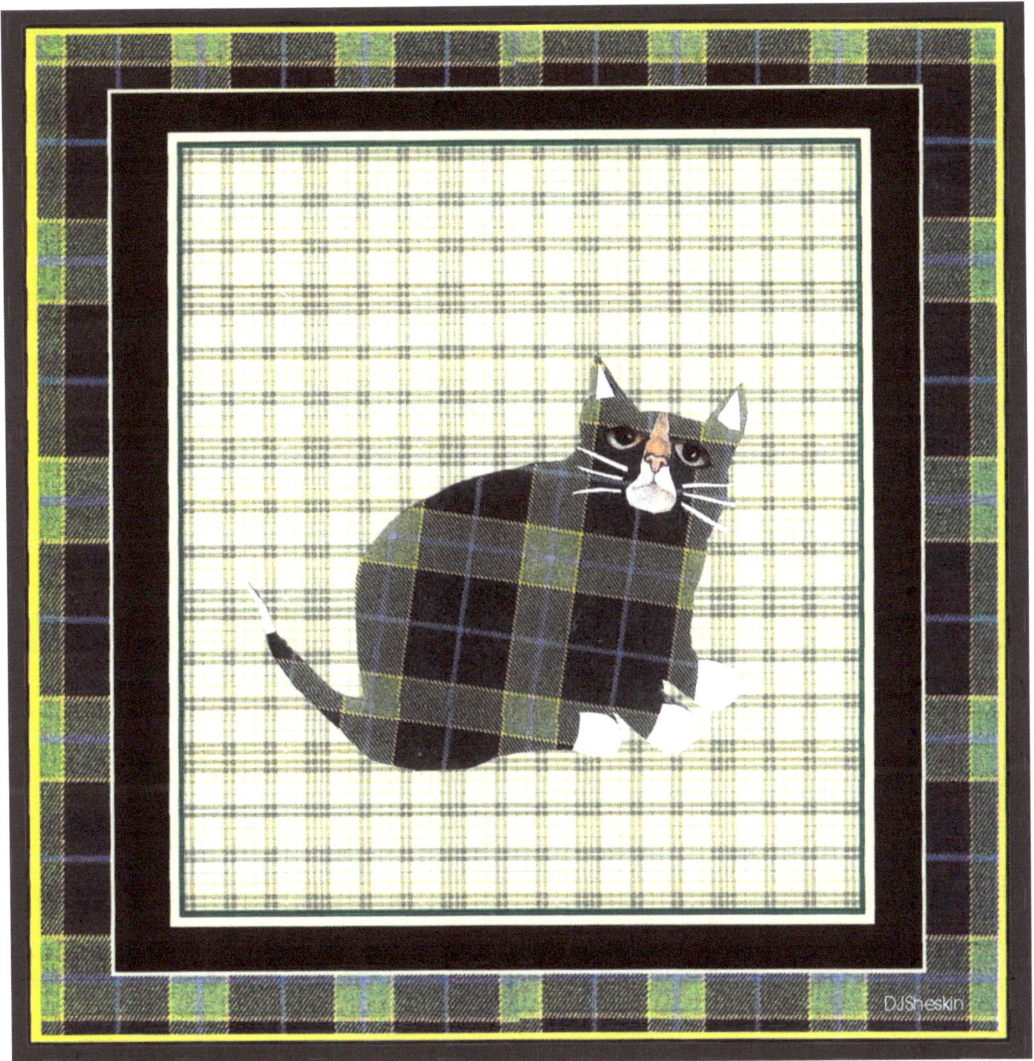

Breed 40: **Peekaboo**
Best of Breed: *Confucius*

A bold, inquisitive cat, the *Peekaboo* can usually be found attempting to gain access to places it's not supposed to be. Because of this the breed does best in a controlled indoor environment where, although given the opportunity to investigate, its ability to get itself in trouble is limited. Although friendly and affectionate toward humans, if given the choice between lounging on its owner's lap or rummaging through a closet, the *Peekaboo* will always elect the latter. The preferred diet of the *Peekaboo* consists of ground up vegetables such as pumpkin, lima beans, and bell pepper, and it is especially fond of sweet potato garnished with horseradish.

BREED 41: FIRECRACKER

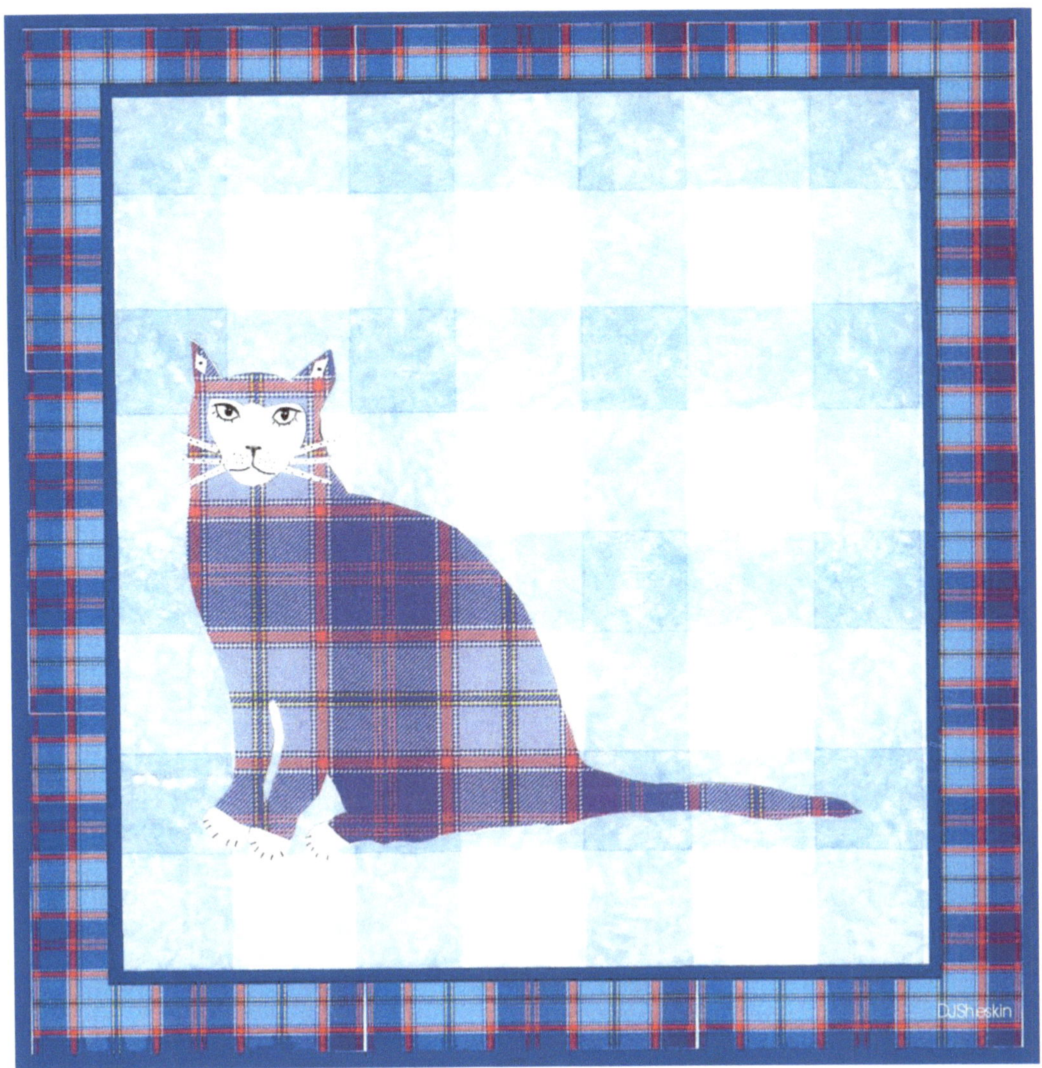

Breed 41: **Firecracker**
Best of Breed: *Sparkles*

The *Firecracker* is an emotional cat that at times can be unpredictable. Because of the latter, the breed is not recommended for owners with young children. *Firecrackers* are often quite jealous of other cats and even humans, to the extent that they can be severely combative toward strange cats introduced into the household and even toward people it views with disfavor. Prized as a show cat because of its brilliant coat and its distinctive white heart-shaped face, the *Firecracker* is among the most expensive of the domesticated plaid cats. In addition to subsisting on luncheon meats and barbecued beef, the *Firecracker* has a preference for flavored liqueurs such as anisette, crème de menthe, Curaçao, pear brandy, and framboise.

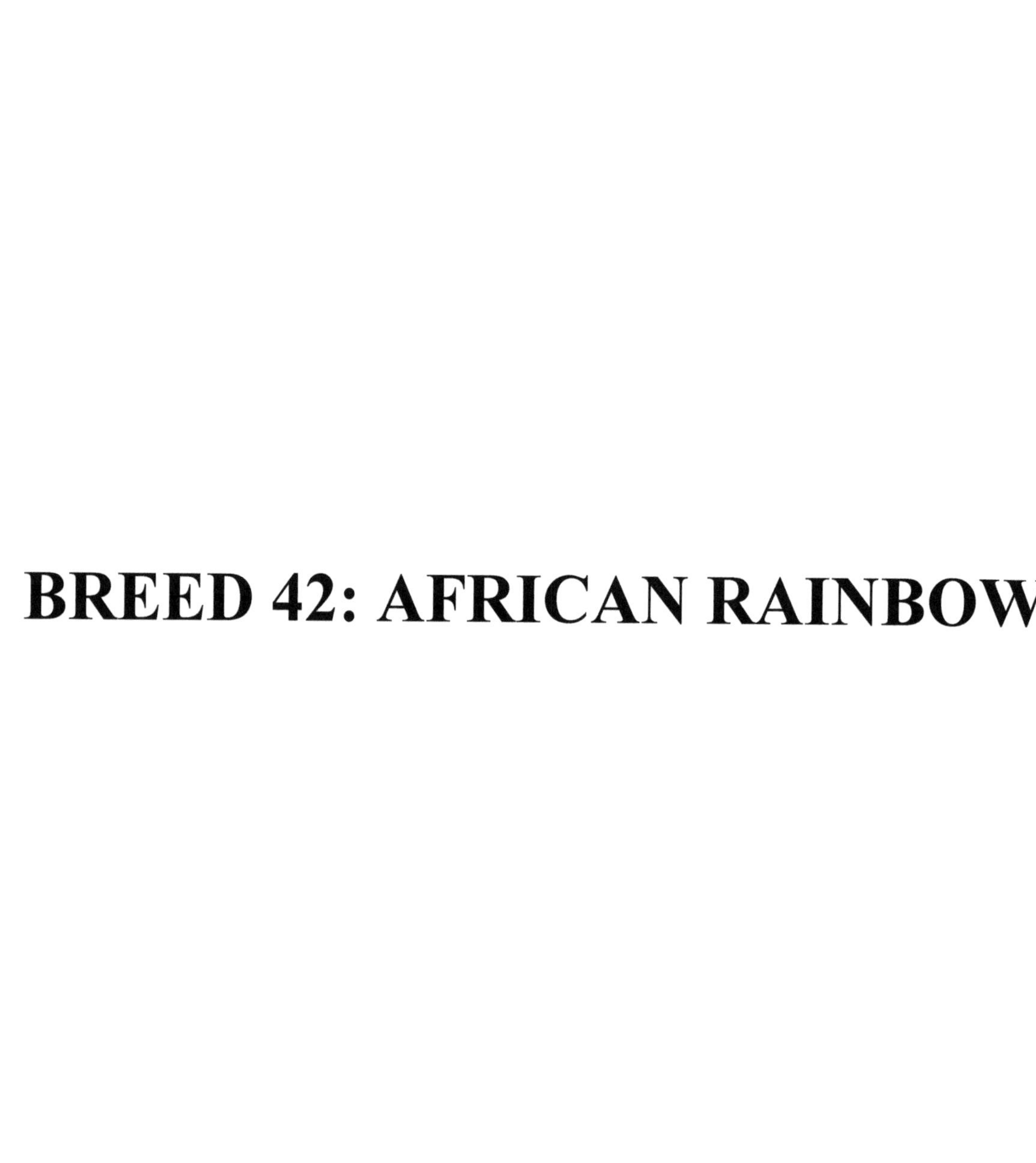

BREED 42: AFRICAN RAINBOW

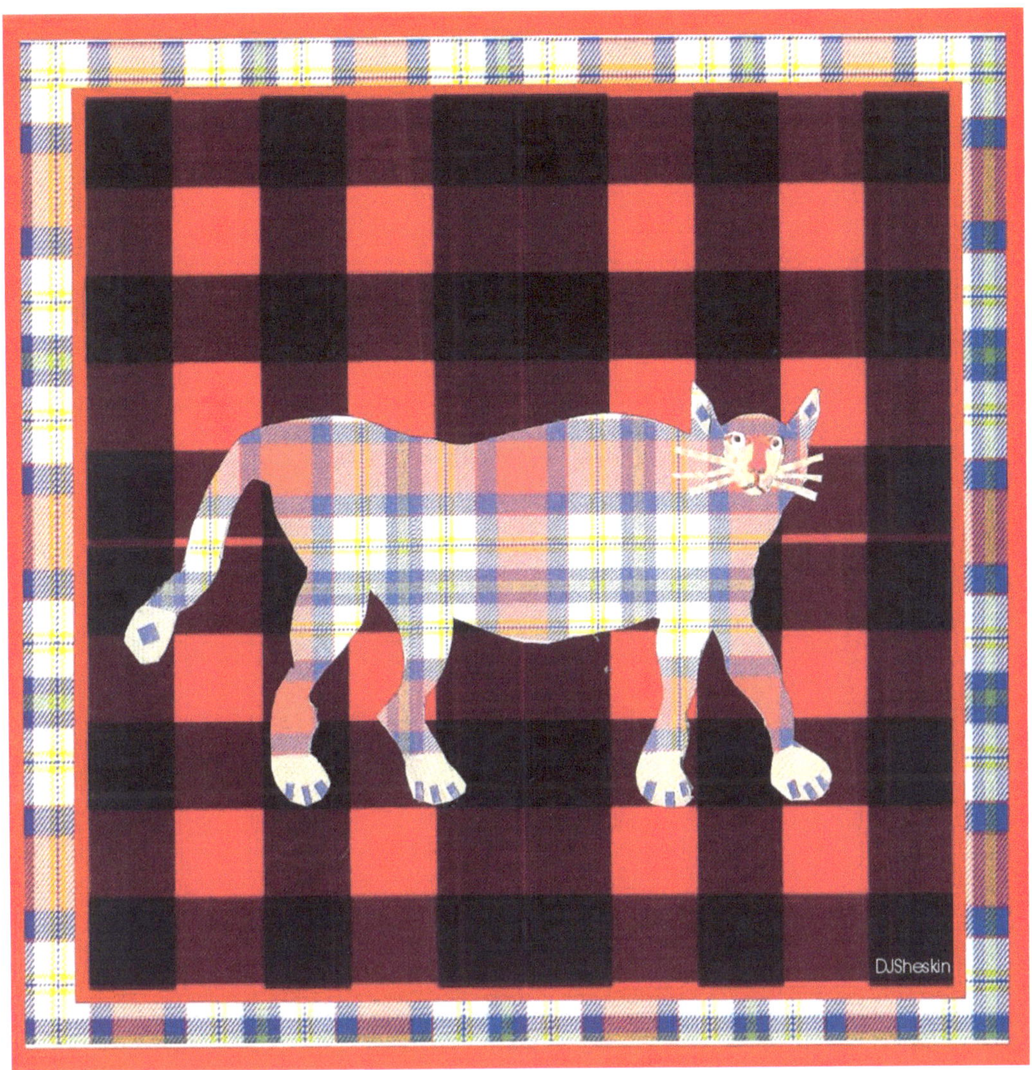

Breed 42: **African Rainbow**
Best of Breed: *Lollipop*

The *African Rainbow* was first identified by explorers in the forests of eastern Zambia in the early 1900s. Domesticated in the 1930s by Swiss and German breeders, it is among the most sought after of the plaid cats. Reclusive by nature, the breed is mellow in temperament. Coveted among collectors because of the stunning pattern of its stripes, the *African Rainbow* is unusually agile, possessing exceptional speed and leaping ability. Like many other southern African plaid breeds, the *African Rainbow* subsists almost exclusively on a diet of chocolate chips, mints, and strudel.

BREED 43: BELLE

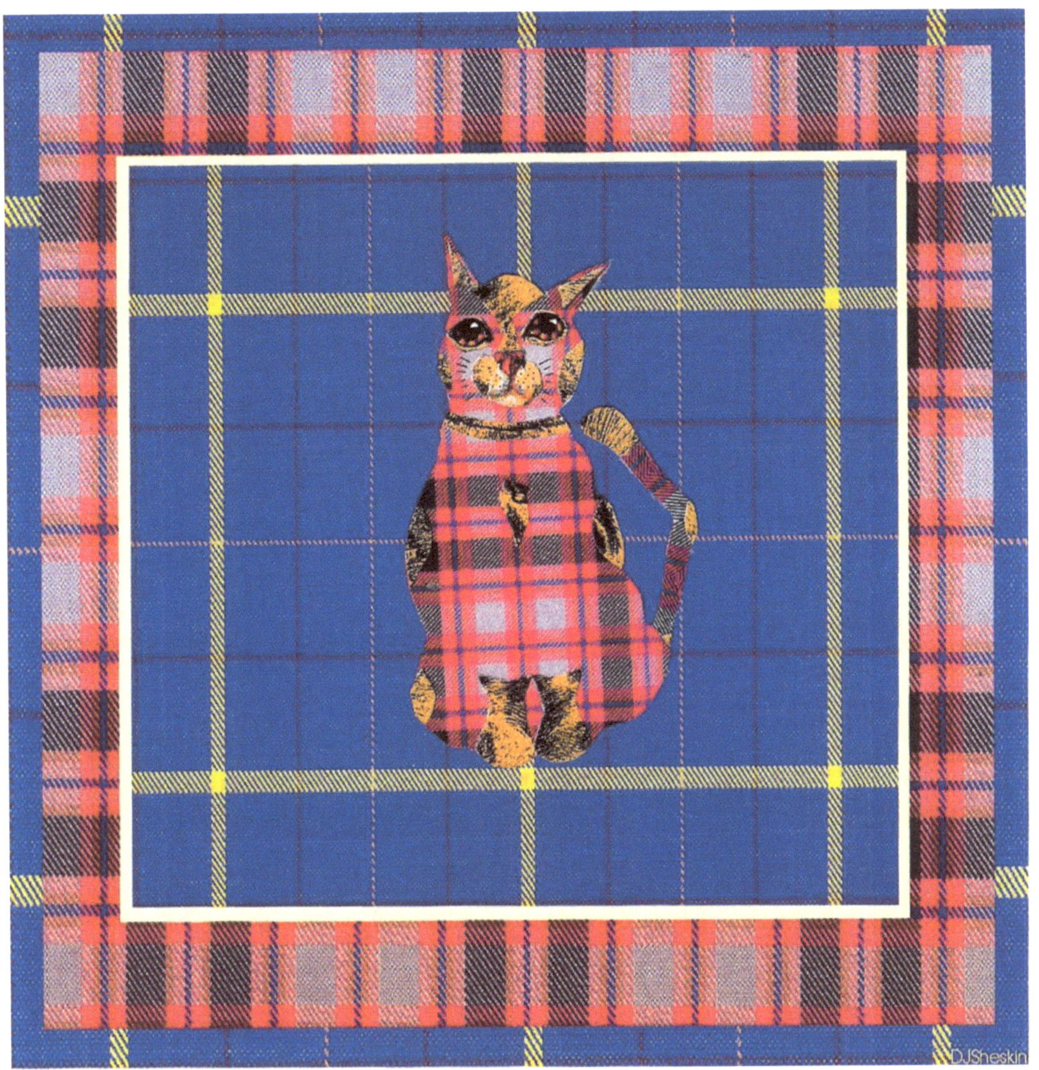

Breed 43: **Belle**
Best of Breed: *Scarlet*

This attractive and even tempered breed was first identified living in the jungles of French Guiana in the early 1700s by British and Portuguese explorers. When the territory was subsequently taken over by France in the mid 1800s the *Belle* was domesticated, and within a few years became a favorite house pet of French nobility. A proud and regal animal, this breed is a meticulous groomer that is famous for prancing about with both its head and tail up in the air. The female *Belle* is the epitome of the devoted and attentive mother, always making sure that her litter is as well groomed as she herself. Recently, breeders have discovered that a diet which emphasizes plantains and red bananas tends to enhance the vibrancy of the carmine and lavender hues which decorate the *Belle's* coat.

BREED 44: WANDERER

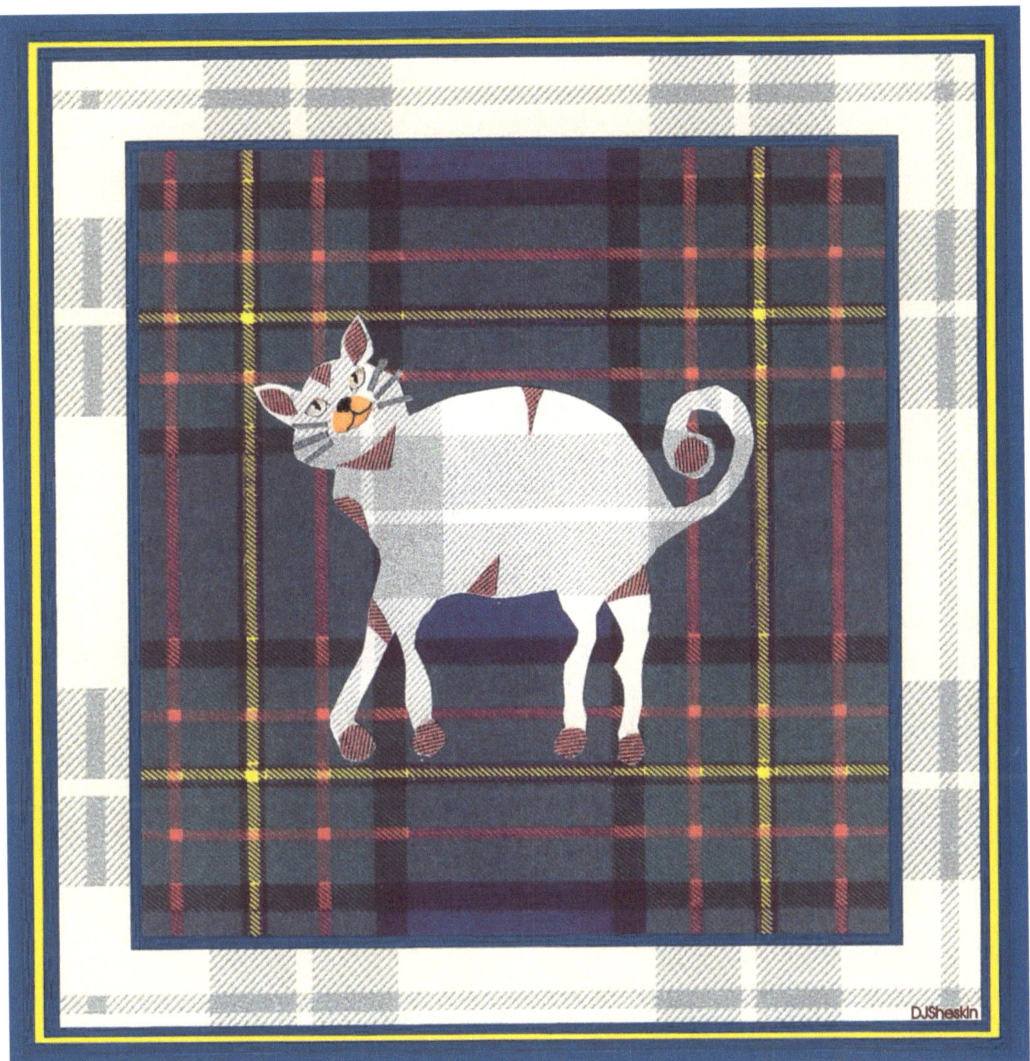

Breed 44: **Wanderer**
Best of Breed: *Hobo*

A bold, inquisitive cat, the *Wanderer* is prone to wander far from its environment. For this reason, it is best kept in a large indoor environment or an outdoor setting which prevents it from escaping. The true origins of this breed are unknown, but it is believed to have resulted from random interbreeding of various solid and plaid breeds over a long period of time. The end product of the latter is a playful, affectionate cat who adores children, dogs, and other cats. The fur of the *Wanderer* is short, exceptionally soft, and exceedingly fine. Periodic rubbing of the fur with a gloved hand is recommended to maintain its sheen. These cats will eat just about anything but are especially fond of hard boiled eggs, cubed steak, and lamb chops.

BREED 45: RIO

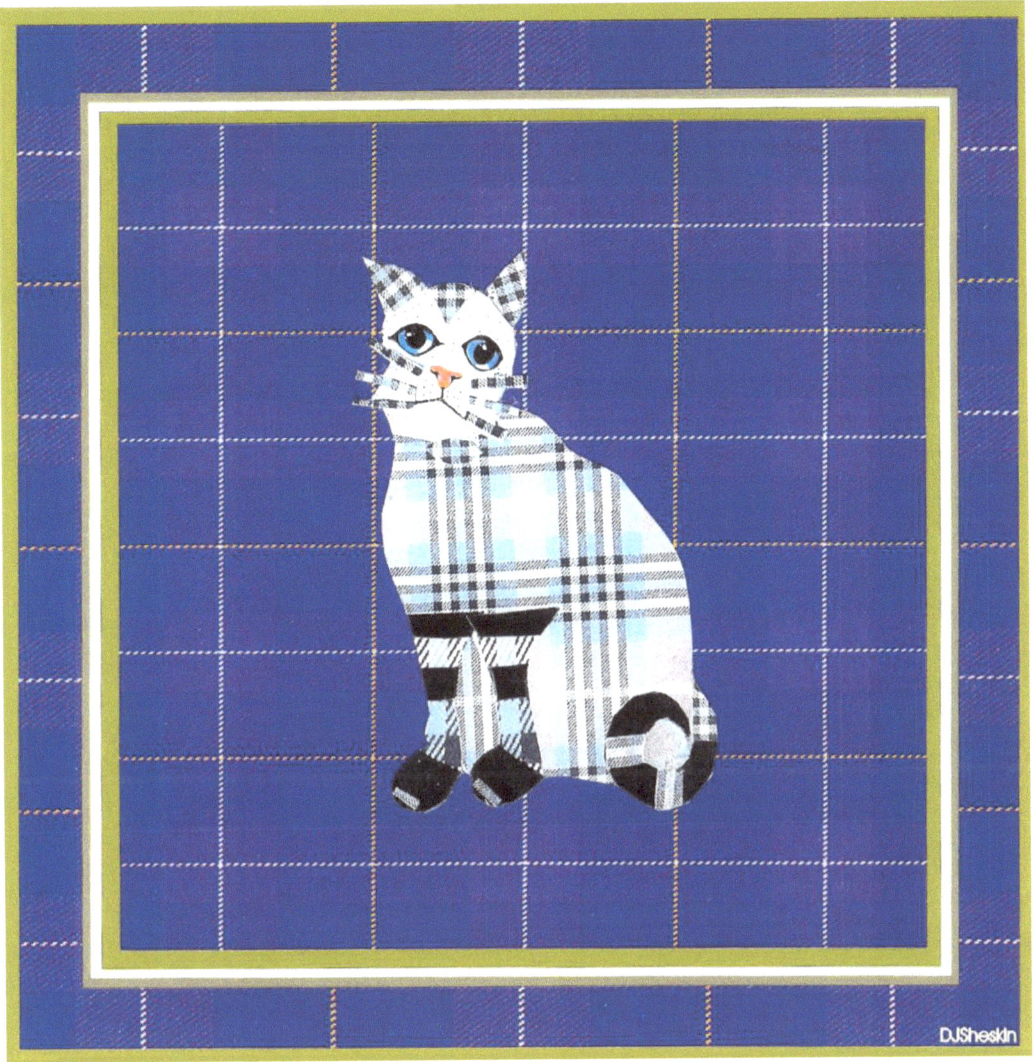

Breed 45: **Rio**
Best of Breed: *Tarzan*

Before being domesticated by Brazilian coffee merchants in the early 1900s, this breed thrived in the jungles surrounding the Amazon basin. Subsequently hunted to extinction by natives who considered the breed's succulent meat a delicacy, the *Rio* is now extremely rare as well as prohibitively expensive for most cat fanciers. In addition to being powerful and agile climbers, males of this breed are excellent swimmers. Noted for the checkered pattern on both its ears and whiskers, the male *Rio* is a gregarious cat that requires regular exercise and attention. The female on the other hand (which has solid black ears and red whiskers) is sedentary, introverted, and reluctant to bond with humans. A typical litter yields three to five kittens. The *Rio's* preferred diet consists of tropical fruits such as banana, kumquat, passion fruit, and persimmon.

BREED 46: ICEBERG

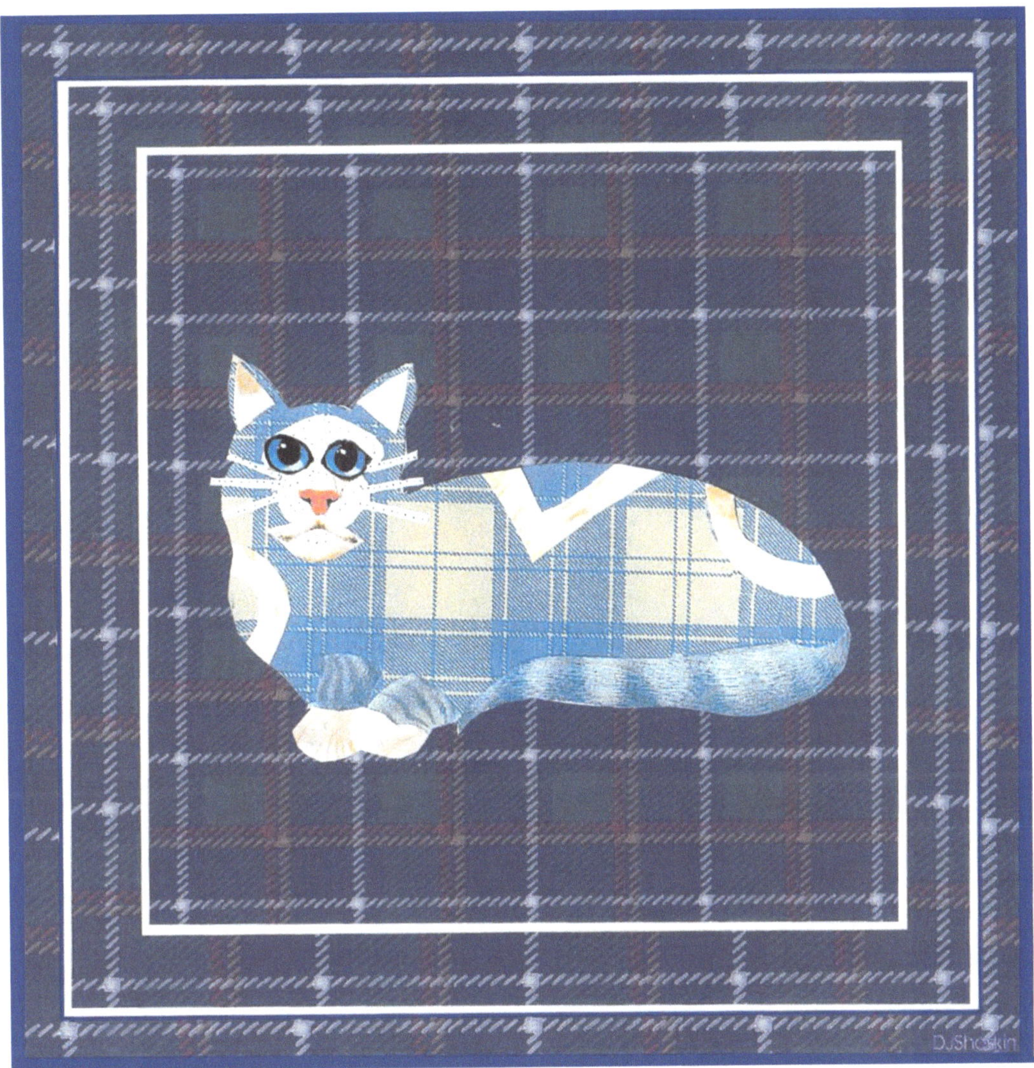

Breed 46: **Iceberg**
Best of Breed: *Snowflake*

The *Iceberg* has a thick, powerful body with four short, thick legs, and round paws with extremely long claws. This arctic cat was domesticated in the 1700s by the Eskimos, and subsequently became a favorite breed among cat lovers in Canada and Greenland. Like many other arctic mammals, its fur is thick and dense, yet unlike most cats its fur is extremely coarse. A natural hunter, the *Iceberg* survives on a high protein diet, preferably meat and fish, as well as such exotic treats as the blubber of seal and whales. Due to its high infant mortality rate when living in the wild, the *Iceberg* is a prolific breeder yielding litters with as many as 15 kittens. Temperament wise this breed tends to be aloof and demands minimal attention from its human companions.

BREED 47: BEHEMOTH

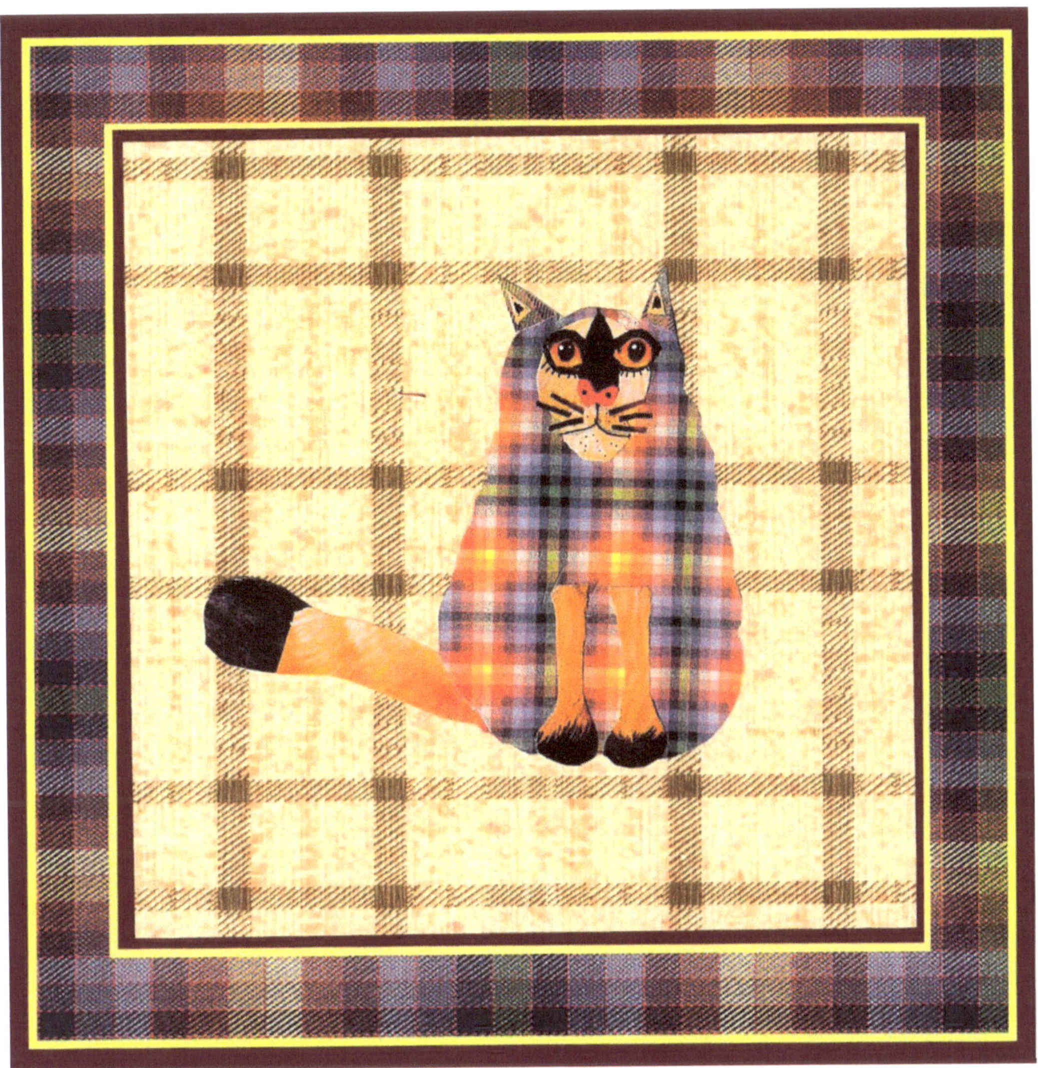

Breed 47: **Behemoth**
Best of Breed: *Samson*

This breed only exhibits its plaid coat during the cold winter months. During the warmer parts of year the *Behemoth* sheds its plaid fur which is replaced with a solid, albeit striking, orange coat. This breed was first identified in the mid 1800s living in remote regions of Patagonia, where it was domesticated by sheep ranchers. The *Behemoth* is powerful cat with a large bushy tail. It is extremely intelligent and can be taught as well as a dog to herd sheep as well as other livestock. Its deep bass vocalizations resemble those of the larger felines rather than a conventional domestic cat. *Behemoths* do best in an outdoor environment and subsist on a diet of small mammals, lizards, and selected vegetables. When domesticated they should be fed a high protein diet.

BREED 48: NEPTUNE

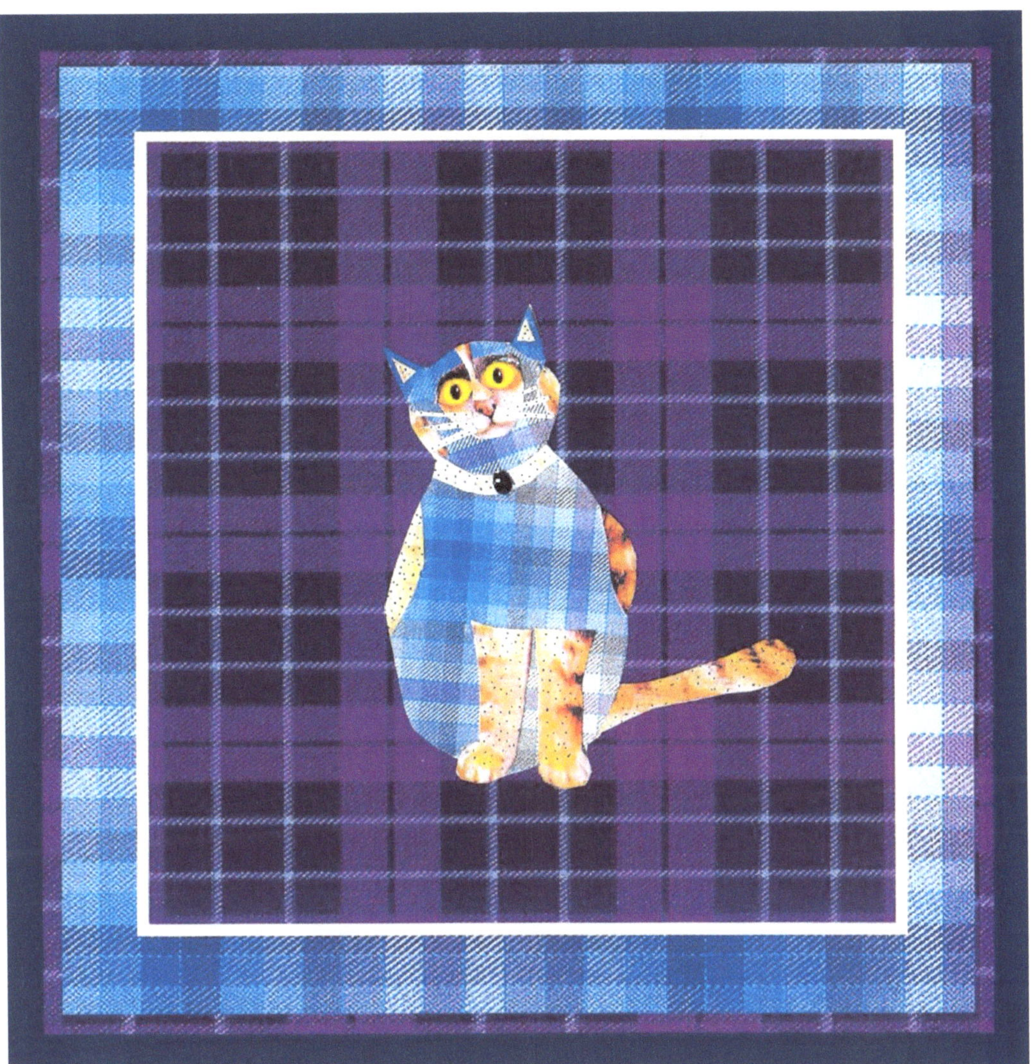

Breed 48: **Neptune**
Best of Breed: *Shark*

The *Neptune* is a breed native to the steppes of Siberia and northern Europe. These are strong, agile cats who enjoy being in water, and are considered to be exceptional swimmers. When domesticated, if possible, they should have access to freshwater or saltwater, and be allowed to hunt for their food, which includes freshwater species such as trout and catfish as well as saltwater species such as sardines, herring, and salmon. Since the *Neptune* living in a natural state is the only feline known to hibernate, when confined indoors during the winter months, domesticated members of the breed should be exposed to high intensity lighting for at least 12 hours a day to counteract lethargy, depression, and prolonged somnolence.

BREED 49: CRICKET

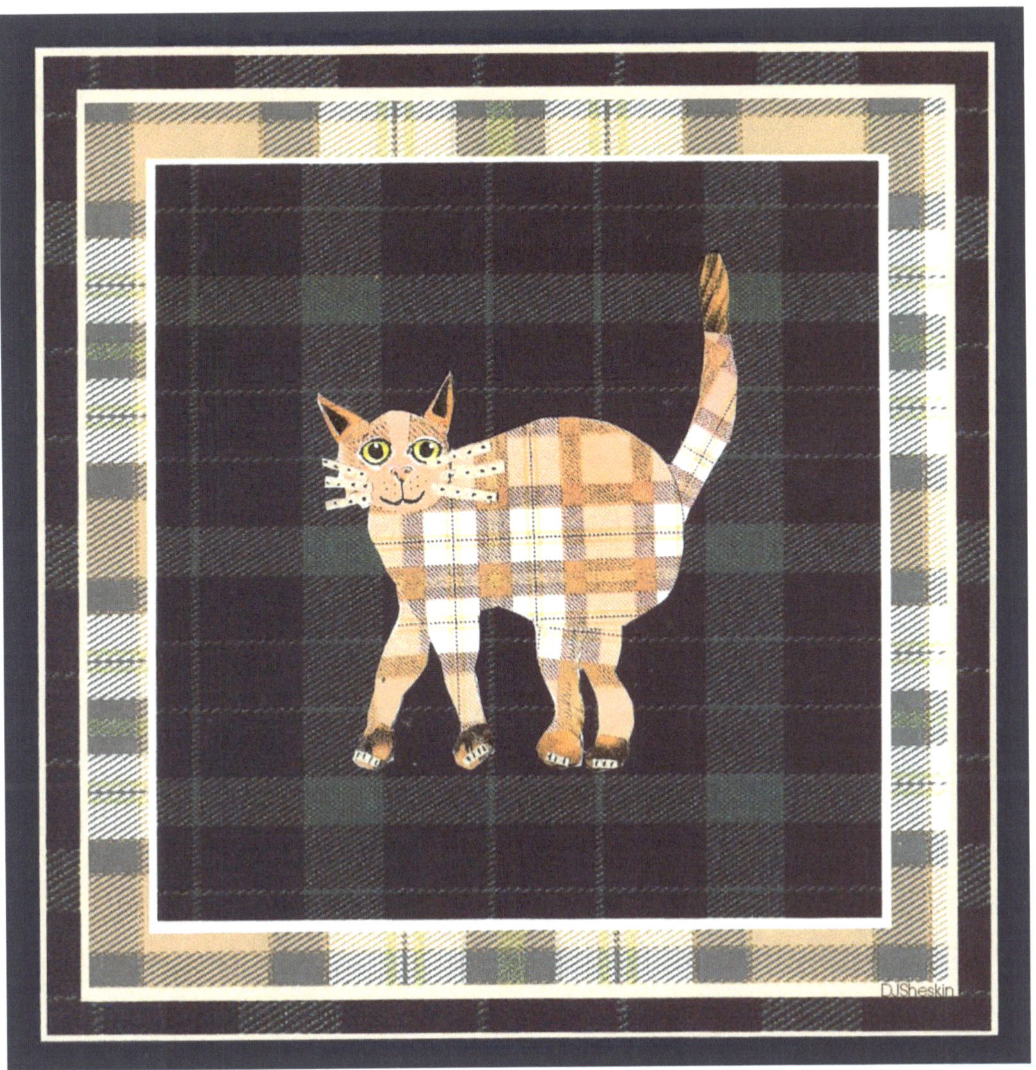

Breed 49: **Cricket**
Best of Breed: *Belly-Button*

This breed is characterized by a compact body with a small head and large triangular ears. An extremely social cat, the *Cricket* is tolerant and loving toward both adults and children. Individuals of this breed have a tendency to attach themselves to one person in particular. Mischievous, intelligent, and incredibly nosy, *Crickets* have to be watched carefully because they are prone to getting themselves into the wrong place at the wrong time. Unique among felines, is the almost exclusive vegetarian diet of the *Cricket*, which primarily consists of veggies such as Brussel sprouts, cucumbers, carrots, asparagus, and snow pea pods.

BREED 50: DAPPLED BLUE

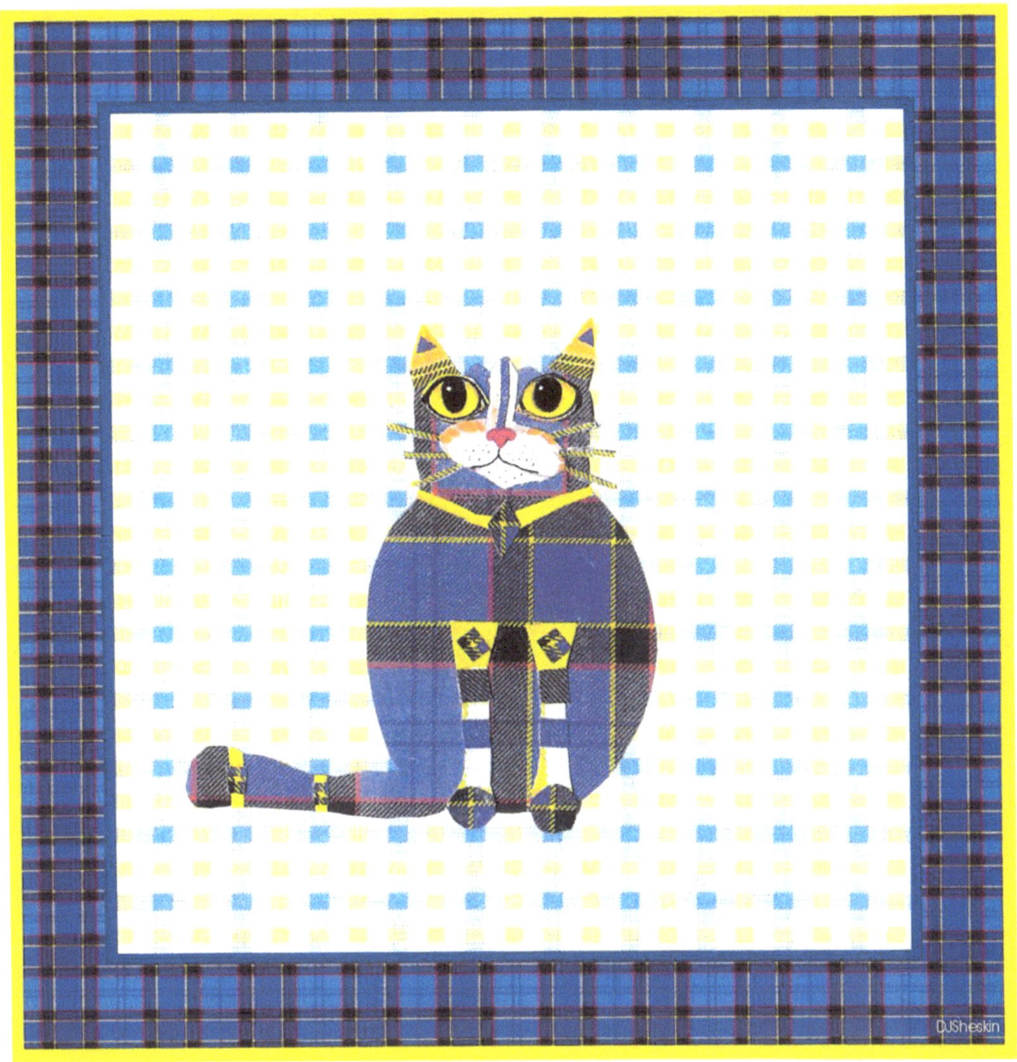

Breed 50: **Dappled Blue**
Best of Breed: *Rascal*

The *Dappled Blue* is an active cat that craves close personal contact with a human companion and an environment which provides a high level of stimulation. Extremely intelligent, these small felines (who rarely grow more than six inches in length) are deceptively strong. Among other things, they regularly use their muscular paws to open draws and cupboard doors. These cats have to be watched carefully, since their high level of curiosity can get them into trouble. To sustain their high level of metabolism, as well as the brilliancy of their coat, *Dappled Blues* should be fed a diet consisting of meat and fowl mixed with assorted vegetables. They especially like prepared dishes such as liver and onions, stuffed cabbage, and chicken pot pie.

About the Author

A writer and self-taught artist, David Sheskin has created a voluminous body of works over the past 40 years. Since 1980, over 30 of his short stories have been published in numerous magazines. A full collection of his short fiction written between 1970 and 2000 can be found in the book *Scientists, Sages and Sundry Other Sinners: The Collected Short Fiction of David J. Sheskin* (2002, Writers Club Press). At the age of 40, David Sheskin created the first of hundreds of works of art he would produce over the next 35 years. His initial works were pen and ink drawings that seemed to spontaneously flow from the tip of his pen onto a sheet of paper. During the 1980s, over 100 of his pen and ink drawings were published in numerous magazines. A full collection of his drawings can be found in the book *Magician With a Pen* (Wingspan Press, 2007). During the 1990s, he began to paint in acrylics, producing a series of folk art paintings and subsequently created new works utilizing the mediums of sculpture and collage. He then developed expertise in the use of digital technology and created, among other things, a large body of realistic and stylized images of cats, dogs, birds, and fish that are notable for their composition and their unique use of color and texture. All of David Sheskin's fanciful, uplifting art can be found in the visually stunning book *The Art of David Sheskin* (Wingspan Press, 2011). Over 100 of David Sheskin's images have been published within the format of calendars (by Avalanche Publishing (*Folk Art by David Sheskin*, 1993) and Pomegranate Communications (*The Owl and the Pussycat* (2009, 2010, 2011) and *Puss and Boots* (2012)), as well as in calendars published in Europe (*Naïve Malerie*, 2004, 2005, 2006 by Ackermann in Germany), note cards, jigsaw puzzles, children's games and digital prints. During the past five years he has developed a form of art he refers to as *Artxt,* which represents the creative integration of art and text. His *Artxt* images (many of which have been published in magazines and exhibited in juried shows) employ the format of a Scrabble board or crossword puzzle to provide a unique perspective on a variety of fictional and topical subjects. All of David Sheskin's art can be found on his three webpages theartofdavidsheskin.com, theartofdjsheskin.weebly.com and artbydavidsheskin.weebly.com.

www.ingramcontent.com/pod-product-compliance
Lightning Source LLC
LaVergne TN
LVHW070130110826
845147LV00002B/227

9781595945778